From Alan &
Christma

Lichfield Cathedral

Frontispiece *Source Unknown*

Born in a CATHEDRAL CITY

Memories Between the Two World Wars

by

Cuthbert Brown

Published by the Author
Jackson's Drive, Charlecote,
Warwick.

First Published 1988.

ISBN 0 9514179 0 8

Second Impression April 1992

Also by Author

MORE MEMORIES 1991.

Printed in Great Britain by
Antony Rowe Ltd, Chippenham, Wiltshire

To my brother, DENNIS,
with whom I shared those early years.

The smiles, the tears
Of boyhood's years,
The words of love then spoken,
The eyes that shone,
Now dimm'd and gone.

Thomas Moore

CONTENTS

AUTHOR'S NOTE

The contents of this book were, originally, intended as a personal record of memories for my own family.

However, as a broader field than family evolved, especially associations with Lichfield, I have been persuaded to offer it to a wider circulation. In doing so it is my hope that many readers will recall and identify a social period which has now disappeared. For others, now and in the future, it may be of interest to read a first hand account of a life from those by-gone days.

I have never kept a full diary (they tended to peter out by the middle of January) and the contents are written mainly from memory but I have had available a vast store of photographs, press cuttings and papers which have been in the possession of the family all these years and from which I have been able to add or confirm many details. Material from other sources, where known, is acknowledged.

I wish to recognise and record the willing help and encouragement from so many people in the production of this volume and thank each one most sincerely.

C. E. B.
Charlecote, 1988.

Chapter One

EARLY MISTS

THESE memories are centred around the Cathedral City of Lichfield in Staffordshire during the period between the two World Wars.

Lichfield, at this time, was a small, quiet market town of gas lit streets leading to a dominant Market Square. It did not relate to any expansion. Overspill from larger neighbouring industrial towns was to be far into the future.

On rising ground just to the north presides the most lovely and ornate Cathedral, one of two in all England with three spires. Known locally as the "Ladies of the Vale" they stand clear and graceful sentinels of the faith, visible across many miles of Staffordshire countryside. Closer they cast their slender reflections deep into the placid waters of nearby Minster Pool, a pool so broad and long that it gives the impression of a river flowing by.

Dr. Samuel Johnson, the great writer of the first English dictionary, was born in this City two centuries before and statues of him and his biographer, Boswell, look down, perhaps somewhat grimly, across the Market Square. The Doctor was proud to have been a Lichfeldian and spoke with high praise of this City of his birth and named her "Mother of the Midlands". Salve magna parens.

The streets of Lichfield had a quiet, yet busy, unplanned charm unfettered then by lines of parked cars. The centuries had moulded the townscape and only a few early vintage models had, at that time, joined the horse drawn vehicles and whistling errand boys. Streets where, without fail, a friend or acquaintance would meet with time to hail the morning and occupy the middle of the roadway without hazard or hindrance.

Along at the Maypole, butter was being slapped and patted into brown paper parcels tied with string, the Home and Colonial would smell of tea and next door H. G. Hall stood, in a blue striped apron, at the door of his meat shop surveying the scene across the Square. In the grocers shops mahogany shelves rose high to the ceilings stacked with Daddies Sauce, Camp Coffee and treacle and the grocer himself in starched white coat bowed and scraped politely from his bacon slicing machine to take the liberty of offering a service to his customers.

In summer in the little sweet and tobacco shop in Market Street everyone gathered for ice cream wafers (twopence for the plain ones — threepence for the chocolate specials) manufactured and dispensed on a plate by the Johnson brothers from a tub hidden by the counter and eaten, not outside in the street but sitting around iron tables in the darkness of their parlour where mirrors lined the upper walls and alternated with colourful advertisements for 'Players Please' and 'Woodbine' cigarettes. Here on winter days hot peppermint drinks and Bovril supplemented lively exchanges about the City Council or local happenings, inquests on the latest disasters at Villa Park, the Hawthorns or Molineux and, in the mornings, the possibilities for Newmarket or Haydock Park.

Further along, Mercer's Sadlery wafted the aroma of rich leather from the bridles, harness and leggings draped around the open door and just around the corner liquorice allsorts, packed loose against the window of Pearks Stores, were offered at four ounces for a penny.

On the outskirts of this town was our home, a mile out from the square to the north west and just where the countryside was resisting urban buildings. From all our windows we were able to look out over the fields and the hedgerows and for that reason we enjoyed the best of two worlds — urban convenience and rural environment.

It was into this home I was born the youngest of a family of four. My sister, Ena, and my eldest brother, John, had arrived nearly a decade before my other brother, Dennis, and myself appeared within fourteen months of each other as early war babies. The age difference of each pair of children tended, at least in the early years, to divide them with their separate interests, yet this did not, nevertheless, prevent them all from keeping together as a tightly knit happy family with caring parents. As time went on this difference receded, and the varied interests of the whole family gradually merged.

This, then, was the back cloth to my early and boyhood years, growing through youth to early manhood at a time when my parents and most other grown ups, were just recovering from the catastrophe of a war which had wrenched them from the security and serenity of the Victorian and Edwardian days into which they had been lulled and were starting to live again their own lives with ambitions and hopes for their young family.

* * * *

The part I played in that early young family comes to me as if through a mist which clears only momentarily and the images, barely focussed, are lost and overtaken by time. Details and reasons can only be supplied much later. But further back into those mists were happenings in which I took part but about which I could not possibly have been aware.

It seems that when I was due my sister would, at her age, know all about the expected event and was desperately keen to have a little sister to attend to. When she saw it was another brother she must have been awfully disappointed; but not to be thwarted she treated me much as she had intended all along and, whenever the opportunity arose, dressed me in flowing feminine skirts and garments and even tied my hair with various ribbons. I do not know how long such treatment lasted but I am sure that, when I was informed of the matter, I would have been quick and anxious to satisfy myself that I had not been deprived of any masculine attributes. And my ego could have been further rebuffed when I was to learn that my parents could not decide on a name for me. They were still undecided on their way to the christening but happened to pass a successful grocer friend, one Cuthbert Wigham, and so one is led to believe, I was baptised a Cuthbert also. I have, presumably, to thank that grocer for salvation from a life of anonymity.

Then out of those time mists appear damaged buildings high above me, wall paper and fire places exposed and strange in the outside sunlight. I would learn, in due course, that this damage related to the aftermath of a stray Zeppelin raid on the neighbouring town of Walsall. Why a child of my tender

The cobbled square with Johnson and Boswell Statues

Market Square — Bus Terminus

Friday Market Day

Market Street from The Square

Market Street from Bird Street

Conduit Street

The Art School (now demolished), Dam Street

age took part in such an inspection I do not know, yet when the mists cleared again, I see huge bonfires with flames reaching, it seemed, to the sky with red, white and blue streamers all about. I was quite able to identify peace celebrations down in the Recreation Grounds.

Through further mists I see myself sitting upon my father's instep clutching with my arms around his leg, my brother is clinging likewise on the other leg and father struggles to walk with us across the dining room floor.

* * * *

But gradually those mists cleared and I emerged from this early childhood to identify myself and relate to my surroundings. My younger brother and I became inseparable as we started growing up together, sharing escapades, tears, smiles and hopes and, later on, the games and the sports that were to become so prominent a part of our lives.

About this time we were awarded a patch each from the main garden to look after. We dug it and weeded it in the approved manner although I do not recollect a surfeit of harvest.

On one occasion father gave us some broad beans which he had left over and which we planted on our patches with much enthusiasm. Frequent visits were made to check whether or not they were coming up, but they failed to appear sufficiently quickly for us and, becoming rather frustrated, we dug them up to see what, if anything, was going on. Of course the beans were going on alright as the root shoots had appeared and were healthily driving downwards. However, after some discussion, we were satisfied the shoots ought to have been going upwards and that we must have planted them upside down. In much haste we replanted them all with the shoots pointing upwards and continued the vigil. In due course the beans appeared through the surface and, once through and having done a 'U' turn, they grew rapidly.

* * * *

But there were never any mists about bedtime for it has always provided a clear childhood picture of happy family security. On dark winter nights we would be upstairs quite early but not always with the intention of getting off to sleep. We were not allowed to have pillow fights but invented plenty of games in the seclusion of the bedroom we shared. We would make wigwams out of the eiderdowns and play Red Indians spying on each other through the little sewn eyelets. In day time these eyelets produced inverted images as we kneeled in the darkness under them. When we were feeling particularly energetic and we had finished our acrobatics over the bedrail, we would play a game which we called 'bulls' whereby we stood on all fours on the bed and tried to bunt the other over the edge on to the floor. Outside the wind would whine and moan along the side of the house and through the lines of telegraph wires along the road side and we would play on quite unaware of the anxieties caused to the grown ups by a gale, a frozen pipe or snow on the ground.

Our bedroom was large enough to play football with a balloon, using goals against each wall yet cosy enough with a fireplace which would be laid when we were ill. On the far wall was an adjustable gas lamp bracket and the fan shaped flame, giving off a peculiar flaring noise, reflected into a picture hung by the side of it. The picture was a coloured print by Robert Spense of George Fox's visit to Lichfield at the time of the Civil War with Fox barefooted in the snow. Watching him are groups of citizens and soldiers, some with rifles and beyond can be seen that the central spire of the Cathedral is almost entirely shot away by Roundhead bombardment. The picture impressed our young minds but we could not understand what it was all about but noted how scantilly dressed Fox was and how cold his feet must have been. It encouraged us to jump gratefully into the warmth of our beds where mother had just placed the stone hot water bottles.

We would be reluctant to be called in for bed on summer evenings but as some recompense, provided we undressed and put on our dressing gowns, we would be allowed to have supper sitting at the open bedroom window where we would watch the wheeling flights of the swallows and look out for some late vehicle to pass along the road. Any movement outside would attract our interest, even the local cat out for his late prowl amused us as he picked his stealthy progress across the garden into the road and along the hedges searching for some unsuspecting victim and quite unaware of the eyes tracing his steps.

Then, not feeling tired, we would ask if we could wait until the lamp lighter came along. He was a familiar figure with a brisk, rather pin-toed walk, holding his rod horizontally much as he had been taught to carry his rifle some years before while serving in the forces. The progressive lighting of the lamps in the direction of the town would inform us that he was on his way and we would see him pause under the lamp nearest to us, raise his rod and hook it on to the ring and chain under the glass. The light would pop up and broaden gradually and by then he would be striding below our window. In later years we would stand and talk to him but he had to keep an eye on the clock as there were many further lamps to light before he could get back home.

But as he disappeared into the dusk we had to hurry and settle down and say our prayers. When we were very young we always said them kneeling, in turn, on mother's knee with hands tight together and head snuggled into her shoulder so that she could hear us saying

> Gentle Jesus, meek and mild,
> Look upon a little child,
> Suffer my simplicity,
> Teach me, Lord, to come to thee.

Then a pause and we would be allowed to whisper our own requirements such as "God bless mummy and daddy and please look after my rabbit".

As we grew older we would kneel independently by our bedsides still with hands clasped and eyes closed and say quite slowly and reverently the Lord's Prayer. This sounded much more grown-up than "Gentle Jesus", although we did not really understand the bit about 'trespassers against us', but we still added our prayer for those near and dear to us and, in later years, I daresay I would add, probably under my breath, a request that I be allowed to get plenty of runs tomorrow! And then mother would come back into the room and fuss with our clothes and check that we had remembered our prayers. Snug and warm and secure in our beds we would confirm with a muffled yes as she stooped to kiss us goodnight and make sure we were tucked in.

Father and Mother

Myself (still in skirts) with Dennis

Mother with her family

Outside '250'

Myself and Dennis

George Fox at Lichfield

Chapter Two

BOYHOOD FIELDS

I HAVE said that our home enjoyed the best of two worlds, but the world of our boyhood related mainly to the countryside about us. Footpaths led across the scene and, with father being so friendly with the local farmers, we were able to wander more or less at will. We soon promoted ourselves from the confines of the garden, pleasant though that was, and set out to learn the countryside for ourselves. Knowledge evolved, yet we never became naturalists. We knew the difference between the nest of a thrush or a blackbird, the separation of their songs high above, the bank where each year the robin built and where the yellow hammers flew along the hedge. We would walk in the stubble with the partridge covey running before us to take wing into whirring flight, we would walk where the stoat ran from bank to bank across the lane and far away a hare would halt his flight, sit upright at the fields edge and look back at us. We would be the first to hear the cuckoo in the spring and know that in July it would be gone. The conker trees — we knew them all, and the growing crops, the field where the cowslips grew, and the frogspawn in the pond on the way up to the big house at Lyncroft.

But looking back now I remember most the corncrake with its persistent summer evening call a few hundred yards up the lane from home. We would hear the rasping sound long after we had gone to bed and we would lie and listen to it through the open window with the call seemingly louder as darkness fell. We would think about the border of long grass around the field by the hedge where we knew the bird had its nest and where we had passed by in the sunshine that afternoon. Little did we know, or even contemplate that within a few decades the corncrake's call would be no more and many of the footpaths and fields we loved so much would be swamped by development.

* * * *

Less than a mile away from home across the fields, was a very large extended tract of land called Pipe Green, so named because of the never failing supply of spring water which was piped to discharge into the brook flowing across the whole length of the Green. Curiously, Pipe Green is still owned, under some remote and unique eighteenth century statute, by the residents of the Beacon Street in which we lived. The rights of the residents are very jealously guarded and administered by a duly appointed Trust Committee and any profits accruing from this management, mainly from grazing fees, are distributed to widows living in the street.

The brook itself, at that time, was well stocked with sticklebacks, although there had been sparse seasons. We often enjoyed fishing expeditions, no doubt exercising some sense of ownership. But before we could set out on some such expedition we would need to gather our equipment which consisted, simply, of a net on the end of a cane handle and a two pound jam jar. Each year we expected to find the items on the shelf in the little shed near the house where we thought we had left everything last autumn but it was nowhere to be seen. No doubt father had taken the cane rods to prop up the gladioli he was tending for the forthcoming Flower Show.

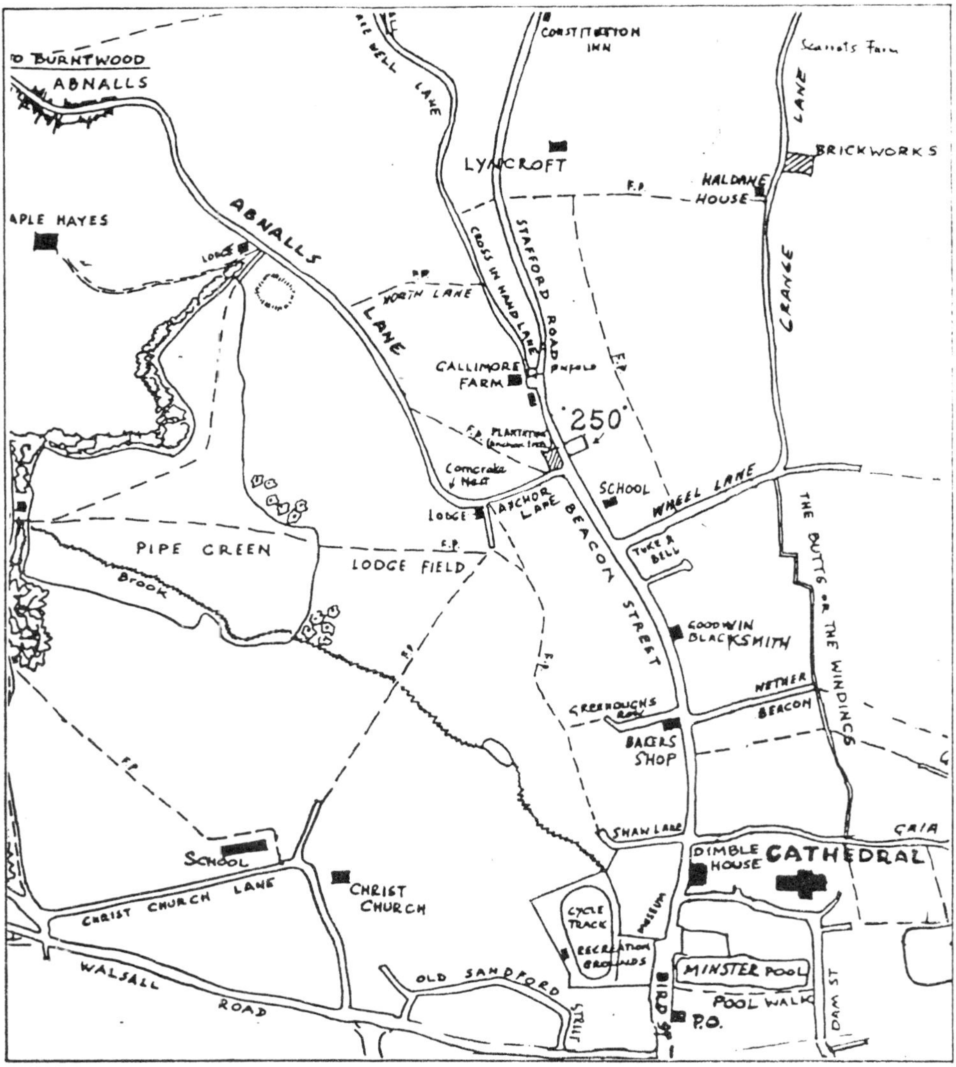

Boyhood fields

So off we would trail back to the house to persuade mother to leave the particular task upon which she was currently engaged to re-supply us with jars. We then demanded string for the handles which was taken from the tin in the kitchen cupboard. Our fingers not being strong or deft enough, mother had to spend further time applying the string to form the carrying handles round the necks of the jars. It never occurred to us to take anything other than jam jars. The essential thing about them being that they were reasonably light to lift up to face level when we wished to inspect our catch which, later in the day, would be seen nuzzling with their mouths against the glass looking back at us from the murky interior. If we had a good day the jars would be totally inadequate to house all we caught. We did once take a bucket but the fascination of watching them was lost as you could only look down over their streamlined bodies. Still failing to find any sign of last year's nets we would be given a few pence to purchase new ones from the little emporium some way down the street. It is difficult to know how the owner assessed his trade in fishing nets for he was always able to produce them.

Finally equipped we would sally forth into the summer morning. Hindsight does not see us setting off in the afternoon — always in the morning with the early sun and a wide blue sky above. Two happy small boys, dressed in dull knitted jerseys, buttoned on the shoulder, heavy material trousers down to their knees, black pumps on their feet, setting off into the sunshine for a morning in search of sticklebacks. We would turn and wave to mother standing at the dining room window watching us with happiness and, perhaps, pride. I have no doubt that sometime later she would approach the window again and look across to the stile to see if we were on our way back and when father came home she would say "I wonder how long they will be?"

Our way to the Green would take us along the lane, past an old Lodge and then down a hedged footpath to the Lodge Field. Over the stile we could see, a few hundred yards ahead, a copse of trees which heralded and stood guard over the Green itself. How many scores of times have I crossed that Lodge Field, southward, with the Green itself beckoning before me? Always with that same eager sense of anticipation and pleasure, often with my sister and brothers, sometimes alone with my dog or with school friends and a bag of old golf clubs ready to knock a ball over the brook into the sunset and, later, many many times, with my wife, Margaret, to see the drumming snipe over the reed beds and to hear the evening songs of the thrush and blackbirds in Leamonsley Wood beyond.

The path along this Lodge Field was wide and cropped and easy to walk along, whereas the Green was a curious mixture of broad areas of cattle grazed grass, (which became our golf fairway), interposed with rougher, tufted grass and, nearer the brook, extensive boggy ground with reeds. This area tended to become impassable at times and, over the years, successive Trust Committees have attempted to drain it into the brook but generally with little success. The whole aspect of the Green was not unlike a common but the enveloping trees, fences and hedges around the perimeter allowed it to have an intimate, even affectionate, atmosphere all of its own.

At the end of the Lodge Field the ground suddenly dipped and ahead was a wide panorama of the whole of the Green. This dip led down to a stile giving access. To assist ascent of the stile there was a large sandstone block, worn and curved down from countless footsteps. It is still in position today but the curve has become even more concave. Once over that stile we were in the Green itself and our pace quickened as we turned left handed across the rough, reedy route towards the brook. Perhaps we ran occasionally in our haste to get there.

The water in the brook was wonderfully crystal clear with a bed of clean golden red sand. Only where the cress grew was there any mud. The banks varied in depth along its course and dropped steeply down to overhang and form small caverns. As we had approached the brook our footsteps had sent tremors through the spongy earth and because of this we would see two or three sticklebacks dart across to the opposite bank — rich dark flashes seeking shelter in the caverns and crevices. "There's one" we would shout in unison, but before we were able to take action we had to take off our pumps and stockings. At one time we would hang them carefully around our necks but we found this such an impediment when we stooped down that we selected a fairly dry tuft of reeds and placed them there. We had to risk cattle nosing about. But once our stockings were off we could not wait to jump down over the bank to feel the sudden shock of cold water enclosing around our bare feet. Shock which took our breath away momentarily but our eagerness to catch the darting forms overrode such setbacks.

Once settled in the brook there was not a great deal of skill in our fishing methods. We merely pushed the net under the bank or into the cress, withdrew it and examined the contents. Usually the net came out full of sand or mud. As the water drained away there could be seen a wriggling movement within it and this was the joyful sign that a fish had been caught. But in these first estatic moments we would be horrified to realise the jars were not only back on the bank but not filled with water. With feverish haste we would rectify the position and eventually the fish would finish up, still alive, in the jar. Thereafter there was always the problem as to where best to place the jar whilst catching the next one. Quite often if placed on the bed of the brook the current would tip it over, or one or the other would accidentally kick it over and we had to start all over again, but the first fish in the jar was an ever to be remembered moment.

Gradually, through the morning, the jars would receive successive fresh catches and the accompanying amount of sand, mud, cress or reed gradually caused the water to become, to say the least, rather foggy and the fish, as they swam around, could only be seen when travelling past that part of the jar nearest to the beholder.

There were only three types of fish involved: reddies, poddies and stoney roaches. The first two were, of course, the male and female stickleback. The reddies so called because of the bright red breast with fierce kingfisher blue eyes. The poddies were larger and less colourful, although a pleasant yellow and silver on the underparts. Size varied according to age and the stage of the mothering process. Reddy and poddy, whenever caught, went into the jar but stoney roaches were another matter. We hated them with their large bull-nosed heads and large gaping mouths. They, too, varied in size but whereas the sticklebacks darted with exhilarating switches and snatches of the body, the stoney roaches appeared sluggish, lay in the sand or wriggled into indentations.

Thus, a morning would pass, carefree and happy, working our way upstream along the whole length of the brook with the chatter that comes only with boyhood. "Got a poddy" or "Just missed a reddy". No thought of anything but our quarry, no thought that it might rain, no thought that the cattle grazing nearby might molest us, no thought, even, that it might well be dinner time.

At very long intervals we may have paused from our task and looked up to glance across the familiar and well-loved undulations of the Green. Gaze across to the wooden paled boundary fence and beyond which, through the belt of beech and sycamore trees, we could catch a glimpse of the stately home at Maple Hayes. Away in the other direction, to the south, could be seen, as ever, the comforting presence of the three spires of the Cathedral.

We did not have any means of knowing the exact time other than the slope of the sun or a vague signal from our tummies but we generally sought out our pumps and stockings at about the right time. On the occasions when we seemed to have time to spare and we had reached the point where the pipe of the spring was discharging into the brook we would cup our hands and drink from it. We would then carefully place our precious jars in a safe position and explore the pathway, overgrown with weeds and nettles, leading out of the Green. The stream overflow coming from Leamonsley Pool found its way down to the brook by a devious route. Years ago the stream had joined the brook through an old brick culvert This culvert was dark and uninviting and we would kneel and look up into its murky interior and wonder how far we dare crawl up it. We never did attempt it but we were always proud to know that one of our cousins had, indeed, crawled up the whole length and emerged at the other end. That cousin, Noel George, served later in the mud of the Flanders trenches when barely seventeen, survived and went on to play in goal for Wolverhampton Wanderers in the 1921 Cup Final against Tottenham Hotspur at Stamford Bridge. The green jersey he wore that day has survived and has even been worn by myself on quite a few occasions when, in a smaller way, I had been chosen as a goalkeeper.

We were never worried about being over on the Green by ourselves and we seldom saw anyone else although a public way ran across it. Possibly we were too intent on our fishing, bending over in the water.

However, we were once afraid that we might have trouble. We were well settled down to paddling upstream when we heard ominous shouting from the other end of the Green in Leamonsley Wood. Now we lived in Beacon Street and approached the Green from the east. In another part of the town was Sandford Street and anyone going to the Green from there would do so in the opposite direction — the west. There had always been some sort of a feud between the younger element of these two streets and we felt they were rather tougher than we were. So much so that although we stood up to them to a degree we tended to hold them in some fear. Even at school, which was midway between us at Christ Church and which, again, was approached from opposite directions, we were always up against each other. At playtime we would form our own football teams to the chant of "Sans are playing the Beacons — Sans are playing the Beacons" continually repeated until the respective teams lined up and the football battle began. The Sans usually won and some animosity must have been generated and, had it come to a fight, I know who would have won. But back to the Green. As we straightened up to hear the shouting we looked up in horror and cried simultaneously "Sans! ". Without discussion we gathered up our jars, collected our pumps and stockings and scuttled off across to the Lodge Field as quickly as we could. We ran barefooted until we considered it safe to sit on the grass, our feet quite dry by now, and put on our footwear prior to continuing on home. Anyone will know the difficulty of running with a jar full of water, let alone one full of fish, and our concern would be to retain sufficient water to sustain the occupants. But they managed to survive and we got them home. Ordinarily we would have wandered home slowly, stopping many times to hold up the jars to see how the catch may have been getting on and to confirm numbers after many recounts.

When we arrived home we would probably change the water, not so much for the benefit of the individual fish, but in order that we could have a clearer view of them as they swam around in their cramped quarters. But they never seemed to survive more than a day or two and we would come down one morning to find their colourless bodies upside down with the stickles protruding horribly. We had many inquests as to why they always died and we were generally convinced that the electric light, which was now installed in the house, under which we examined them was the main cause. Later we amended this view to think it may have been the introduction of tap water into their systems. Much later, in fact decades later, when my son went through the same fishing stages he went about it in a much more efficient manner and even succeeded in prolonging life in captivity to the extent of several generations.

* * * *

We took a keen interest in the farming activity in our local fields. The area was, mainly, part of the Maple Hayes Estate and the owner, W. W. Worthington (of the Brewers) had erected a large wooden 'W' on all his five barred gates of which there were many. The land was husbanded by the Gallimore family — known to us as just 'the Gallies'. Their farm, Pinfold Farm so named because of the adjacent pinfold (which still exists today), was only a few minutes away from us along at the junction with the Cross in Hand Lane. There was the father and three sons, Bill, George and Jim. George had a wooden leg but it seemed little impediment to him as he slashed the turnip tops, the cauliflowers or built stooks in the cornfield. He usually wrapped a sack around the stump of the artificial leg to prevent it sinking into the soft earth. He didn't bend his leg at the knee when walking but swung it out in a wide arc at each step. How he crossed the field picking up sheaves thrown to the ground by the binder, and keep pace with the others is hard to conceive.

The younger brother, Jim, was in charge of their three shire horses and for that reason he was the only one who wore breeches and leggings — sometimes he didn't bother with the leggings. The others were always dressed in long heavy Derby twill trousers with leather belts sagging below their waists and, when in the fields, they tied the traditional binder string just below their knees, presumably to ensure clearance of their turn-ups from the soil. No-one else ever handled the horses and it was always Jim who was behind the plough or the mower or driving the cart to market. This cart loaded high with baskets of cauliflowers, heads all facing outwards, was an inspiring sight. We only saw it because it was loaded up in the evening so that they could make a pre-dawn start for the Black Country markets next morning. It would be well into the afternoon before they returned empty. When eventually the farm progressed

Gallimores

Boyhood Lane!

This photograph of the Anchor Lane says it all. The way to the Green and Christ Church School top left. In the centre the stile where we rolled our ball. The plantation is bottom right with the Maple Hayes signpost.

(St. Mary's Centre Photograph)

to motorised vehicles it was Jim, naturally, who transferred from the horses to the driving cab.

Jim was a faithful member of the choir at our Parish Church and walked down every Sunday to both Matins and Evensong, a total distance, there and back each time, of some four miles. His journey, in his blue suit, took him past our house and we would watch him go by with a curious plod leaning forward with one arm bent behind his back. This sedate Church-going figure was quite different from the one we knew out in the fields — pulling and straining on the reins as the pair of horses snorted and brushed against the hedge in a tight corner over by the pond.

* * * *

One of the highlights of the summer was the corn harvest. Word would soon spread that "Gallies are cutting today!". Gallies would have already contacted my father as he did a lot of shooting and along with a few others formed a squad to shoot rabbits as they fled from the ever lessening area of standing corn.

We used to go along with father. A width of the corn around the perimeter of the field would have been cut by scythe the day before to allow Jim, with his binder and two horses, to start their circular cutting tours. The guns took up positions at each corner of the field. The other Gallimores would be progressing around stacking the sheaves thrown out by the binder into stooks — two rows of four sheaves stacked against each other. As they passed by a gun at each corner they would stand for a moment and give an up-to-date assessment as to where the rabbits might be in the corn.

Suddenly, though, there would be an almighty ear piercing detonation from just above and in front of us. It was father shooting at a rabbit which had poked its head out of the corn. But from the ensuing shouts and banter we assumed he had missed it. I think he invariably missed the first one. From then on there were roars and bangs and frequent intervals as rabbits left the corn. "There's one", someone would shout as a rabbit ran for the sanctity of the hedgerow, leaping high over the sheaves and bang would go father's gun followed by sporadic bursts from the other corners of the field and, quite often, we would hear the spatter of pellets as they spread through the leaves of the hedge line trees.

By this time Jim, as he controlled the stamping and nodding horses, would be standing up out of his seat shouting and pointing down into the corn. How on earth he, the horses, his brothers, or the groups of spectators missed being hit I do not know. Indeed, on one occasion one of the bystanders in the corner of the field by the stile did appear to have been hit as blood had appeared on the lobe of her ear. Some concern was expressed as she called attention to the blood now transferred to her finger and she was solicitously led away from the field of fray by her supporters. But there was no break in the barrage. As to whose gun was responsible it would be difficult to say but I think she was heard to mutter as she went "something would be done about it". Rumour has it that the next morning my father and one of the other gunners met on the post office steps at 9 o'clock to renew their gun licences, presumably just in case.

But the afternoon went on. The victim rabbits were laid out — with sympathetic sighs from the women and children present — in ever increasing rows.

At one stage a different slow moving form appeared at the edge of the corn and I wondered why father did not have his customary blaze at it. Amongst some good humoured banter Bill went over and prodded it with his foot. Apparently it was a hedgehog which was allowed to go on its slow way into the safety of the hedge.

The climax of the afternoon was fast approaching for only one width of corn remained standing. At this stage the brothers gave up stooking and walked nearer to the binder where it was considerably safer. Jim was still standing up shouting and gesticulating. Suddenly there appeared a general exodus of rabbits from the corn and they darted out in all directions amidst even more shouting and pointing. The banging and roaring reached a crescendo but these late rabbits knew what they were doing apparently, because most of them, in this last minute stampede, reached the safety of the hedge in all the confusion. I have no doubt a cheer was raised as the last one leaped the final sheaf and the guns became silent. Then Jim, with a knowing smile on his face, would take the horses from the binder and lead them to the green grass under the trees. He then retraced his steps to where the others were dividing out the rabbits.

Meanwhile my brother and myself would have been collecting as many of the cartridge cases as we could hold. They held a peculiar fascination for us; not only was their smell exciting but the stiffness and the newness of the shells was attractive. We would insert our fingers in them and hold them up to make a peculiar clacking sound as the brass heads knocked together.

When father was ready we would walk proudly home with him, his gun at the slope arms, with his fair share of the rabbits looped over the barrel and down his back. We would not see those rabbits again until mother produced them as rabbit pie. We loved rabbit pie and were fascinated by the various forms of the bones we picked, especially those kite shaped ones of the shoulder blades.

Chapter Three

PASTIMES

We always seem to have found our time fully occupied. I never remember being at a loss for something to do and I was certainly never bored. This applied to the whole of the family and I am sure that my father, with all his activities, would have preferred a day of twenty-five hours at least.

There was no television, of course, and even the radio or, so called, wireless was very much in its infancy and reception, although a thrill, was usually poor. The only receiver available at this time were crystal sets. These were chancy affairs because, even with an aerial half way across the garden, reception was dependent on the cats whisker, a little bit of spiralled wire, being twiddled on to the correct part of the crystal itself which had the appearance of a very small piece of coke. Having achieved that position you usually sat with your elbows on the table, holding the headphones to your ears and saying "shush" to the room in general. When valve sets and loudspeakers were introduced the whole family could share reception and listening status rose in proportion to the number of valves in the set and the size of the loudspeaker.

But "listening in" did not take up a major part of time indoors. The Christmas Annuals, 'Chums', 'Chatterbox' and the others kept us supplied with reading material and this was supplemented by the weekly editions of 'Tiger Tim's Weekly', 'Bubbles', 'Rainbow'. These progressed to 'Modern Boy' and the far more sophisticated 'Children's Newspaper'. Father insisted we had this publication and, of course, as always he was right for it certainly brought to us a sensibly presented and wide aspect of the current affairs going on in the world. We then graduated, via the 'William' books to the more classical volumes provided from the well stocked shelves of our teaching Aunty Annie and those Ena and John left about. They had a run, about this time on Sapper's Bulldog Drummond and it was also their choice that introduced me to a life long enthusiasm for Sherlock Holmes whose later group of stories had just been published.

Interposed with this sporadic reading, especially in winter and those evenings when it was dark early and we could not go out after tea, the table would be cleared and we would become engaged in a variety of indoor activities. Card games with mother and the rest of the family were always popular. Mother was a keen Whist player attending most of the local Charity Drives and she taught us the basic rules of 'second player play low' etcetera. From this we were soon proceeding into the rudiments of Auction Bridge.

We enjoyed table tennis on the dining room table. We played so long and often that, as with lawn tennis, we knew each others play and weaknesses and exploited them to the full. But there was far too little space at either end of the table which prevented us from standing back and really opening our shoulders and this restricted our methods to rallies of well placed half volleys. There was a further hazard as the open coal fireplace was adjacent and I have seen dozens of ping pong balls land in the flames where they frizzled and melted down to nothing despite our feverish efforts to rescue them.

Meccano was quite a favourite pastime and played a prominent part in our indoor activities. Elder brother, John, had been a keen enthusiast and had built up a considerable stock pile of various components. These were handed down to us, and we set about constructing our own models, yet I never obtained complete satisfaction from the system mainly because I felt the individual shapes did not always relate to the model I had in mind, although the introduction of coloured pieces and Dunlop styled wheels did improve the appearance. My brother was far ahead of me in technique and he advanced into models incorporating clockwork motors and complicated bevelled gear systems while I was content to screw an empty swiss roll box on to a basic chassis and steer it round the table legs on the kitchen floor as a delivery van. There was an excellent shop in Lichfield where a whole counter was set aside for Meccano parts. Thus, as we made our models we would list the further items we needed and obtain them, the next time we were in the town, much as car spare parts are purchased over the stores' counters today. Mr. Ernest Jones, who with his brothers, owned the large shop at Bore Street Corner with a large motor garage attached, attended, in his grey dust coat, to our lists with extreme patience but may well have raised his eyes to the heavens when, at last, we trudged out of his shop.

* * * *

Outside, and left to our own resources, our range of pastimes was extensive yet simple. We did not spend much time on swings or home made seesaws and 'tick', although popular, was restricted to the playground of our early school, but looking back now I think it remarkable to realise the hours spent with even a hoop. These hoops were about three foot in diameter and were made of either rod metal or of wood, with a fixed guiding handle or only a chock of wood to propel them along but all requiring a degree of skill to handle them and to obtain the best control and, in turn, the very high speeds which we considered essential.

Imagination also played a part. For instance, we could rush about, each holding a stout stick about eighteen inches long held at either end and were certain, in our fanciful minds, that it was a high speed motorbike handle bar we were holding and with imitatory piercing roars of racing exhausts and gear changes, we were convinced we were riding in the Isle of Man TT races. The actual races were followed with much interest each year. About this time twist grip thottle controls had been introduced and we twisted our sticks with outflung elbows to give even more reality to our fantasies.

Another of our inventions was the "winter warmer". Upon particularly cold days we would raid the shed for a couple of empty cocoa tins even tipping out some of father's nails to achieve our purpose. A number of rough holes were pierced in the ends with the nails and a hammer, old rags stuffed into it and then lighted. Holding the tins at arms length we rushed up the road and quite soon the rag would smoulder and exhaust dense volumes of horrible smoke trailing behind us. The smell was awful as, presumably quite oblivious to the possible asphyxiation of passing pedestrians, we pursued each other up and down. Eventually the tins became so burning hot that we were forced to drop them and obtain some sort of insulation before continuing. The rag eventually burnt out and we would toss the tins, with some satisfaction, into the dustbins before starting to do something else but, at least, by then our hands would be very very warm, even if slightly blistered.

Riding our scooters was always a pleasurable occupation. We had various models through the years and it is small wonder that when we came to ride bicycles we had little difficulty in achieving our balance. Mother found that the trouble with scooters was that the soles of the boots on our left feet wore out so much more quickly than those of the right. Tricycles, too, of varying sizes and designs came our way, but it was not until we had the chain driven variety that we were able to attain anything like the speed we had in mind. Again, we found ourselves going round corners on two wheels and even on the straight. I suppose we were rather dare-devilish because, whilst on holiday at Rhyl, where tricycles were hired out on the promenade, we were firmly requested to go slower and to use all three wheels.

In addition to these shop-bought means of locomotion were the trucks and the soap boxes of our own amateurish construction. The difficulty of producing them was lack of raw material, particularly the best type of wheels. We could not be sure, either, that some of the timber we ear-marked would not be wanted for some project father had in mind. Any model we produced had to be a two seater, but steering and propulsion were always the chief problems. Steering was achieved with heels against the pivoted front axle and locomotion by the one sitting on the rear pushing along with his legs and sitting backwards. In the event we usually finished up careering down some very steep incline, quite out of control, hanging on precariously until a wheel came off and the whole thing overturned, throwing us one over the other onto the bank. Anxious, at first, we would pick ourselves up, burst into some uncertain laughter and take the pieces back into the yard to consider building the next model. All these occupations would go on up and down the garden path or, more often, in the roadway outside. Here we were not faced with any heavy traffic and we, more or less, had the scene to ourselves. A horse and cart would come along occasionally yet cause no undue inconvenience and the few buses or cars at that time did not hold our games up for long. Although, I do well remember convoys of khaki lorries trailing northwards, presumably they had come over from France, but where they headed we never worked out. There were also, on occasions, convoys of T model Fords going through. They would have landed at Liverpool and be on their way for distribution in the south. My sister has reason to remember them for on one occasion she was riding home on her bicycle when she apparently moved across the road so much so that one of the Fords, braking hard, veered away into the kerb rather heavily. Unfortunately one of the nearside wheels collapsed and black wooden artillery type spokes were strewn along the roadway. Two small boys watching beat a hasty retreat to a nearby vantage point from which to watch and hear the subsequent negotiations when my father arrived to see what all the clatter was about.

Soon afterwards, I suppose, we would be out again spinning our tops. We spent many hours with them. I was never very good at top spinning and envied the amount of spin and movement my brother and others could achieve. Furthermore, he could start the top spinning with a flick of the fingers and thumb whereas I had to screw mine into the gap between the setts in the gutter, wind the string of the whip laboriously round and then, with a sharp pull, start the thing going. We did not stand stationary, keeping the top spinning, but gave it a resounding crack and careered off after it a score or so yards on to give it further impetus. When other children joined us seven or eight tops would be spinning all along the road.

If there was little traffic on the roads in those days there was, of course, even less in the sky and the appearance of an aeroplane was an event indeed. So rare was it that whenever a plane was heard in the vicinity a shout would go up "Aeroplane!, Aeroplane!" to ensure that everyone would rush out of the house to see it. Graham White had enthralled Lichfield some years earlier by making a forced landing nearby at Fradley when competing in the £10,000 Daily Mail Air Race from London to Manchester and he had spent the night at the George Hotel whilst awaiting repairs. As boys we had always thrilled to aircraft and such feats as the first flying of the Atlantic by Alcock and Brown in their Vickers Vimy Biplane, and those of Jim Mollison, Kingsford Smith, Amy Johnson and, later, the winning of the Schneider Trophy outright was very much to our hearts. Alan Cobham brought his flying circus to local fields and we were able to examine the machines from close quarters and watch with awe as someone 'walked the wings'. With all this interest in flying we gradually became accustomed to more planes in the sky and we could observe the progress in their size and construction over the years.

* * * *

Great fun was always enjoyed whenever a tennis ball was available. For one of our games we made use of a high brick sidewall of a building just higher up the street. That building had been erected by my mother's people who were Master Bakers and it was their proud new bakery. Above the windows 18″ white heavy letters had been painted 'HYGIENIC BAKERY'. These letters provided us with ready made targets for the ball to hit, one by one, in succession. If a letter was missed you were out and had need to retire to the end of the queue to await your further turn. All sorts of variations were introduced for subsequent rounds such as left handed throwing or throws under one's raised leg. A very simple game but, in those less sophisticated days, one that gave many hours of laughing play and some skill.

Another game played with the tennis ball, or preferably with the heavier sorbo type, was located at the side of our house where there was a paved area. A small pebble was placed about 9″ from the house wall and standing some eight feet back we threw the ball at the pebble, the ball bounced on to the vertical face and then back to the thrower. Points were scored for direct hits on the pebble and if the return was not caught your innings ended. Ena and John, being older, were more efficient and we were content to sit on the nearby doorstep, watch them and count the progressive number of throws made. But we eventually gained the same skills and were soon diving about making one handed catches which, I have no doubt, gave us basic practice for future fielding in the slips.

Quite often after tea on spring and summer evenings the tennis ball would come out again for us to wander a little way up the lane to the stile where

The Anchor Inn (now demolished), Beacon Street

The Anchor Inn and Anchor Lane (now Abnalls Lane)

Cottages Beacon Street, taken down for road widening

The brow of Beacon Street hill

other neighbouring children would have gathered. Here a permanent row of holes had been scoured out on the verge and were used year after year. Again the game was simple. Each was allocated one of the holes and the ball bowled across the lane. Then everyone would disperse except the one in whose hole the ball came to rest who would collect it and call to the others to freeze. In these positions they would be targetted by the throwing of the ball. Points for a hit were accumulated and the process started again. We played on until the holes could hardly be discerned in the gathering dusk and, even if hailed by parents, we would generally hope to get in one more roll of the ball. Then, when darkness fell and we had escaped being called in, we would hurriedly arrange a game of 'Dicky Dicky shine a light'. Here again the rules were basic and related to the game of hide and seek in the dark. An old bicycle lamp was produced which, in those days, would be lit with a paraffin wick. Those with the lamp would be given time to move away and hide but they had to ensure the light was able to shine on an adjacent surface. In due course the following pack would set out and on their call of "Dicky Dicky shine a light" the lamp would have to be shone. Eventually, but not always, the lamp was located and the sequence started again.

* * * *

There were times when, perhaps, we had lost our ball, or the wheel was still off the truck, or our scooter needed a new tyre; yet we did not mind for, even if we did not feel like a walk over the fields, there was plenty of other things to do. At such times we were able to fall back on the pleasure and the sanctity of a dense spinney, just near and almost opposite our front gate. That spinney had something of a local history all to itself for, at one time, it was the site of a public house called the 'Anchor' and this gave its name to the lane running alongside it and which lane, incidentally, was that along which we would set out for the fields and beyond. Older residents of that time remembered this public house and there are photographs to prove its existence. Apart from that there was no evidence on the ground at all to suggest it was ever there. Certainly not in this modern day as the particular area is part of the roadside verge and partly the garden of a recently built dwelling.

To transgress further one is tempted to wonder why the public house was ever pulled down. Personally I think it was removed because it was something of an eyesore to the Squire up at Maple Haynes who would need to see it every time he returned home frome the station or wherever he happened to have been that day. He owned the land and could, before those days of planning law, demolish a perfectly good public house if he so wished. Mind you there were plenty of other public houses lower down the street towards the town, so much so that it was said, and there is evidence to the effect, that there used to be some dozen such taverns between here and the market square which led to the unloyal and unkind suggestion that the Cathedral City was one of pubs, parsons and the other profession.

However, demolished the public house was and in its place trees and bushes were planted on the low ground with a brick wall and iron railings around the perimeter. Thus, when my brother and myself reached boyhood here was a ready made jungle in which our imaginative minds could be given full rein. To everyone else it was known as "the plantation" but to us it was briefly "the planty". Once over the wall, which flanked my mother's property, we could be lost in a world all of our own. Slipping into the undergrowth we could crawl and explore unseen by anyone. In places it was quite dark. From time to time we could climb up and peer over the wall to see if anything was going on in the road outside. At the far end the blue rounded coping of the wall was about at eye level and many has been the time when, standing on tip-toe, we have seen the Squire himself swing round the corner in his black Rolls Royce limousine on his way to his stately home, sitting in the back behind his peak capped chauffeur, he in a bowler hat staring absent-mindedly our way and thinking more, perhaps, about the game dinner waiting for him up at Maple Hayes rather than worrying, or even being aware of, two small boys watching him from behind his own brick wall where they were trespassing on his land.

The Anchor Lane, now called Abnalls Lane, along which he travelled led also to the village of, strangely called, Burntwood and at one stage the Squire erected a very ornamental signpost at the side of the plantation. On it was depicted a flaming wooden torch in bright colours which, I suppose, apart from being a pointer to the direction of Burntwood, would amuse the many guests on their way to house parties at Maple Hayes. But meanwhile, having tired of exploring our planty, we would collect white snow berries from the bushes and carry them in our caps to the step by the gate at home and amuse ourselves throwing them into the roadway to see how long they would survive before being squashed by passing vehicles. When they had all succumbed we would play five stones or noughts and crosses in the sand with our fingers and wait for mother to call us in for tea.

Looking back now it is surprising the number of people who walked by as we sat there. Today a walk of a few score yards is almost unheard of, yet then many people passed our gate as they walked the mile or so down to the City and back again, perhaps two or even three times in the day. Weather made little difference.

Sometimes we would desert the step and crawl up under some bushes where our front garden flanked the footpath and we would continue to watch people go by from that higher vantage point. Our faces, as we lay, would be on the same level as those of the passers by but they were quite oblivious of us inches back under the bushes.

Many years later when I too had need to be in town each day learning my profession, I became the owner of a fairly large dog — a Setter. This dog also sat in this very same spot under the bushes waiting to welcome me home. He, too, watched the passers by only inches from them and they, still not realising his head and eyes were following them through 180° as they passed along. Had they but known he was there they would probably have taken avoiding action and edged nearer the kerb away from his sentry post.

* * * *

Sometimes when we arrived home from school mother may have cycled into town to attend the Women's Institute. The Institute was something of a new venture about this time for up until then this feminine meeting had been known as the Women's Club. They owned a hall of their own in Lombard Street which had a plaque above the entrance door bearing their monogram 'W.C.'. Their legs were pulled so unmercifully that they were forced to fall in with the more acceptable initials of the Women's Institute. Mother would have left jam sandwiches for us on the kitchen table and these consumed, we would make our way outside again. On some such occasion we might have walked up to the Pinfold by the Cross in Hand Lane and spent some time straddling along the top of the walls before wandering down Beacon Street to look in , briefly, at the school playground. Then we would find ourselves at the windows of a small lorry body building works, Tuke and Bell, in Wheel Lane.

Although interested in the lorries our main aim would be to try and pick out a neighbour who worked there as a carpenter. But we could not see him amongst the wood shavings by the benches so our interest wained and we moved further on. We soon reached one of our regular visiting places — the Blacksmiths. We never ceased to be fascinated with the goings on here as we stood in our usual spot just inside the large sliding door. Bill Goodwin, known to his friends as Goddin, and his son Alf were very typical smiths of that time. Heavily built, swarthy, shirt sleeves well rolled up, with leather aprons slit at the front, they were easily recognisable as father and son. They were always busy and never did we pass by but there were at least two or three horses in the shop, some the heaviest of shires, smaller ponies or fine hunters. We quickly came to be aware of their ponderous strength as Alf's 14 lb hammer thundered and rang down to the target on the anvil and flakes of molten red metal sprayed away on to the rough blue brick floor. There would be the usual happy exchanges with each other or with the many passers by, and then, if there was a lull, they would smile across at us and enquire "how our dad was going on". Father knew them well because he handled all their insurances.

We never ceased to wonder at the production of the perfect shoes from an ordinary looking flat length of iron cut from the rack on the far wall of the smithy. The bar would be pushed into the hot embers of the coke fire and old Bill would stand looking towards the street as his body swayed sideways and down to the well practised rhythm of pumping the handle of the bellows, the hand of his free arm placed on his waist. Sometimes there seemed to be a faraway look on his face during those few minutes, perhaps, seeing us at the door he was thinking back to his own childhood or, more likely, he was only thinking about the tea which Alf was just brewing in the corner, but then he would stop and stir the bar in the fire and rummage it in the glow. With much, seemingly abortive clanging on the anvil, alternated with heavy blows on the bar, the shoes would be gradually shaped.

It surprised us that the horses were always so willing to have their hooves offered up. There seemed to be no resistance, as with 'ups' and 'whoops', 'come on my lad or my lady', Bill grasped the tuft of hair at the fetlock and lugged it into a comfortable position between his legs. Satisfied, amongst the unforgettable smell of burnt hoof, the shoes fitted correctly, they were dipped into the waiting tank of water where, much to our delight, they sizzled and steamed before being nailed on with those peculiar square-headed nails hammered home to an unmistakable hollow thudding sound. The protruding ends were taken away with quick twists of the claw hammer before the rasp trimmed the whole of the hoof now propped on the stout iron tripod. With a clatter of the new shoes on the brick floor Alf would turn the horse round and tie it up to the rings along the wall before stroking and bringing out the next one from the line.

By this time mother would be on her way home and it was not long before she appeared over the hill cycling her slow way. As she approached we would leave the smithy and cross the road to wait on the kerbside for her. Then, as she drew level, we would run along by her side for the last few hundred yards to home. Her bike was very much the high framed variety of the day with no cross bar but a long curving stiffener from the handle bars round to the saddle tube. This enabled ladies to mount or dismount with due decorum and without embarrassment. There was also a special guard, laced over the rear wheel from mudguard to frame, which prevented the skirts becoming entangled in the spokes and the chain was enclosed in a gear case for the same reason. But all these details were probably never noticed by mother for, to her, a bicycle was a bicycle and she may not even have used her bell. On one occasion it was recorded that she picked up someone else's bike and rode it all the way home and when the error was pointed out commented "I thought it seemed different". But we would help her push the bike along the path by the side of the house and take it on to the bicycle shed before going indoors where, from her bag, she would take some small toy she had bought for us from one of the stalls down at the market.

Chapter Four

MY FATHER

My father, John Samuel Brown, was born at Sandfields, Lichfield in June, 1879 and most of his ancestors have been traced to this area. His father was an engineer at the adjacent water pumping station and had married a girl from nearby Redlock, Mary Headen.

As with other neighbourhoods in Lichfield at this time Sandfields was surrounded by open fields at Redlock, Dovehouse and Harehurst leading up to Aldershawe and father, as a boy, would roam these fields with his dog, 'Bran'. Although their home was near the Birmingham Road in the parish of St. Michael the family attended for worship at Christ Church which was some distance away near the Walsall Road. Father had joined the choir of this church as a boy and sang with them continuously until some sixty years later. To attend church he would have to walk across a wide tract of land known as the Moggs. This land was common ground and had broad accessible areas through which flowed a very lively brook. Footpaths were plentiful with a connection into the town itself through a narrow alley way into Bird Street just opposite its junction with Market Street. So extensive was the area that all the visiting circus pitched their Big Tops within it together with the side shows, menageries and caravans. However they were forced to transfer to the open ground at Levetts Field when the Moggs was given up as an open space to make way for the new Friary Road system.

From an early age my father took part in the many and varied sporting activities of the Town. Within a stones throw of his home was the Cricket Field, a fine county ground with a vista of the Cathedral beyond. He would wander down and become absorbed in the high class cricket, watch the flannel and sash clad players at practice and talk to the professional cum groundsman, Watson, as he emptied the grass box after the ponies long haul across the outfield with the mower. Eventually he himself became a playing member — a left hand bat yet a right hand bowler — and continued to take an active part in the Club throughout his life. In due course John, Dennis and myself played many years of cricket with him.

He also became an especially keen member of the City Cycling and Athletic Club and was secretary over many years near the turn of the century organising the many social events and club rides over the whole of the midlands area — the local villages in the evenings and weekend runs as far afield as Dovedale, Warwick, Stratford and the Cotswolds. A clock presented to him in 1901 for services rendered still chimes in my room as I write. As a sprint racer he was, I understand, outstanding and told of races in which he took part at the Aston Grounds before it became the Football Stadium of more recent times. He also took part in the Athletic section and was proud to have participated in the Stafford to Lichfield Marathon Walk — some sixteen miles. When he gave up an active part he retained a keen interest and helped and encouraged many local athletes.

I suppose with all these interests, his connection with so many different associations and a position in a prominent solicitor's office he became well known in the City and came to be called affectionately 'Sam', sometimes 'Bish' and, later, simply JS.

He was to meet a young girl from another part of the town, Alice George, the youngest daughter of a very successful master baker whose shop and bakery was at the corner of Greenhough Row and Beacon Street. They were married at St. Chad's Church on August 18th, 1904 and set up home at 214 Beacon Street. Just before the 1914 war, with an increase in family envisaged, father built a larger house in the same street numbered 250. That house was to be my home for over two decades and it was referred to affectionately as simply 'Two Fifty'. It still is today.

To say that my father was a remarkable man is very much an understatement. He must have been a most versatile and energetic person to all those with whom he came into contact. In the business world so wide apart as Law, Rating and Insurance, in the many charitable and voluntary organisations he either founded or supported, in the sporting scene of the district, in Freemasonry and, of course, in the domestic connections of his family.

But without any doubt his wife and his family came first. His main aim and his ambition was for all of us to succeed. No matter what personal or financial sacrifice he had to make, whatever effort, encouragement, time or thought needed, he never failed to provide. Although of limited means and at a time when financial grants were sparse or even non-existent he ensured our education and training at University, Training College or by costly indentures. But in return he asked for one thing. That we always gave more than a one hundred per cent effort in all our undertakings. "It is that little bit extra that counts" he quoted throughout his life. But whereas he *demanded* this little bit extra it was he himself who *earned* the love, respect and regard with which he was held by us all — *earned* by his considerations, his actions and his way of life towards us. We all responded to his call. I may have taken longer than the others to realise what was expected and some of my light hearted approaches to early school life may have confirmed this, but in the end he ensured that the message broke through and, thanks to him, I too, have been able to enjoy a successful professional career and, perhaps, that little bit extra upon which he insisted helped also my sporting activities.

His determination to ensure success was illustrated when it was reported to him, that the maths teacher at Ena's school — the original Girl's High School at Yeomanry House in St. John Street — was not satisfied that she had reached a standard sufficient to take a qualifying examination for Training College. Most concerned he talked with the headmistress and the teacher who both remained adamant. His answer was that if she had not the required standard now then she would achieve that standard in time for the examination and where could he find tuition to this end? Three persons, in addition to father, came through the matter with credit. Firstly the maths teacher who, realising father's determination, offered to supply the extra tuition, but on the condition it was given in holiday time, and at her own home which was in the village of Yoxall some eight or so miles from Lichfield. In those days this would be a problem as there would be no public transport reaching the village. The second person who gave that little bit extra was Ena. Not only was she faced

Father

Alice George at the time of her engagement to father

with the problem of getting to Yoxall, eight miles away, every day come rain or shine for at least fourteen days, there was, of course, the extra study involved. But she would get down to the extra work and she would cycle those eight miles! Mother comes into the story in two ways. First by supporting father in finding further cash they could ill afford and secondly, as a young girl in her teens could not be expected to cycle all those miles on her own, she would, though time consuming, cycle with her each day Thus for those two weeks they cycled to Yoxall. Ena reached the qualifying standard and came through the entrance examination to college to start a career in physical training in line with the sporting instincts of the rest of the family.

Father started his career, and was for many years, in a solicitors office but eventually turned to rating and valuation which became his eventual career. But in his own time he took on multifarious duties and positions which were essential to him financially and to add to all this he built up insurance and most of his friends and contacts relied on him to provide that service. I suppose that, had he been starting his career in this modern day and age he would have set up a limited liability company termed something like 'Sam Brown Enterprises Ltd.

In addition to all these things he took up voluntary positions with other associations in the city of such varying interests as The Small Bore Rifle Club, The Greenhill Bower, The Chamber of Trade, The Allotments Society, the local Butchers Association and the Scott Institute (where he played a useful game of snooker). But, perhaps, the most significant of all was the enthusiasm and help he gave in raising funds to build the new Cottage Hospital in Lichfield and, to complement it, the setting up of the Hospital Comforts Fund. Tens of thousands of pounds were raised under his Chairmanship and, as I have already written, he had time to cherish and look after his family.

* * * *

My father was not superstitious, apart from always avoiding the number thirteen, but he did allow himself to have a number of rituals or habits all of his own making. Every Monday tea time, for instance without fail, he turned up with a whole variety of attractive cream tarts and iced cakes which we called fancies. These included cheese cakes, a delicacy of puff pastry with a central cavity filled with lemon curd. He always selected one of these and it amused us to see him cut it in half horizontally and invert the top before eating. Another of his rituals was to provide a bar of chocolate, or some similar confectionary, which he placed every Saturday night by our bedsides, when we were asleep, so that it was there for us to enjoy before getting up on the Sunday morning.

Supper time provided unfailing procedures. Father would collect a bottle of Guinness from the crate where they were kept in the pantry and place it on the hearth near the fire to warm. We could never understand his reason for doing so. Eventually, having located an elusive bottle opener, he would pour the contents into the tumbler held at arm's length and at eye level and watch, with interest and satisfaction, the forming of the head. Also at supper time there was the detailed dissection of a tomato. Father never ate the skin or the seeds and he went through a regular and lengthy process, watched with fascination by his family around the table, in such a way to segregate the fleshy part.

There were other occasions when he would suddenly appear with one of his favourite bloaters. The rest of us were not too keen on them and so he would carry on and cook the thing for himself. He liked them best grilled over an open fire. This was effected by using a metal grill, the two halves of which closed together to grip the said bloater in between and the whole held over the fire continually being swivelled for the flames to catch the whole of the body. Unfortunately this action caused a certain amount of spluttering and grease tended to fall on to the grate and the hearth. He was far from popular when the cleaning schedules were undertaken the following morning.

Another of the rituals was the old coat always worn to feed his poultry. The coat must have been years and years old and why it was necessary to be worn every time has never been explained. Even if we had visitors he would not divert from his custom and he must have been totally unaware of his image as he hurried across the garden with corn and buckets to the fowl pens. As with all his interests, father engaged in the keeping of poultry with enthusiasm. Our garden was sufficiently extensive to allow him to have a small orchard for his carefully selected variety of apple and plum trees, a vegetable area and four interconnected and enclosed runs for the hens.

I remember the first pens he erected, which even he admitted would hardly have obtained planning consent. We helped him in the construction. It is the thought of these pens which always brings back to me the smell of tar. He would never set a piece of wood in, or near, the ground without daubing it with a liberal coating of tar usually mixed inadvertently with a quantity of soil. Tar was also applied to the felt roofs in similar liberal quantities. The gluey morass was kept in large tar pots which kept falling over and it was applied with very long handled brushes. Our main duty when helping in these constructions was to hold a brick on the reverse side of the plank he was nailing to make it solid and thus, avoid the splitting of the wood. Imagine our guilty horror when the nail came through inches away from where we should have been holding the brick.

During these building and carpentry sessions many incidents arose which would be talked about and embroidered down the years. The hammer or the pincers could never be found at the crucial moment yet, usually, turned up close at hand under some piece of timber; the chisels were, it appeared, always blunt and father suspected we used them as unofficial screw drivers. A correctly sized spanner was never to hand as, one after another, they were offered to the nut. All these little things worried me at the time but now, since I have undertaken many such tasks during my married years, I appreciate they are the rule rather than the exception.

But the life of these pens was limited because, having attended the Royal Agricultural Show at Derby one afternoon, father announced, over tea, that he had purchased a new purpose made fowl pen. In due course it arrived and was fully approved by the family. There were three compartments, the first two dry scratching areas and the third formed the night quarters containing perches and nesting boxes. But these boxes were unique to us because they had a contraption whereby the hen, with a coloured ring of identification on her leg, once having entered to lay could not get out again until released and until her egg had been

Father — Racing Cyclist

and Marathon Walker

Early Cricket at Lichfield

registered in the laying book. After the first laying season the novelty wore off somewhat and even father's enthusiasm faltered and the hens were allowed to leave without permission.

He then experimented with various breeds of birds and in this way we were able to learn all about the Red Leghorns, White Wyandottes, Light Sussex and the rest. Eventually he started rearing cockerels for showing purposes and entered them in the large show at the neighbouring village along at Alrewas. The White Wyandotte Cockerels were magnificent birds with their cream bloom and flushed heavy red combs. But such show conditions was not obtained easily. The day before the show they would need to be shampooed. This operation had to be undertaken in the back scullery and if ever anyone has witnessed such an operation they will realise the smell of wet warm feathers can never be forgotten nor, for that matter, will they forget the extreme difficulty in handling, let alone controlling, a wet and angry cockerel. After rough drying with towels the birds were left overnight in all their white glory each caged in a large basket either side of the kitchen fire. A final fluff up with a large pair of bellows just before the show would complete the preparations. But on one occasion fate took a hand. Father had retired to bed with one last look of admiration at the two birds and his mind may well have been on the morrow when, at the show, he would be handed the red First Prize Certificate. But on descending the next morning he was horrified to find that, in the night, one of the baskets had toppled over, the cockerel had escaped and attacked the other. In the ensuing fight blood had been drawn in sufficient quantities to ensure that the overnight prize winners of white plumage had turned themselves into red spattered and bedraggled feather caked objects lying exhausted on the floor. After that experience father withdrew from the show ring.

It was about this time that I became aware of the stupidity of hens. Quite frequently they got out into the garden and we assisted father in trying to get them back, in what ought to have been a reasonably straight forward orderly procession, but which usually turned into a fracas because the birds simply would not go where you wanted them to. The result was the slight ruffling of father's calm and many a time I have seen him forced to throw his trilby hat at the 'dratted' things. Such a mild expletive as 'dratted' was, no doubt, tempered by the presence of mother in an adjacent part of the garden. But, I suppose, for all their faults and stupidity the unmistakable and satisfying cackle of hens, after laying, was always fair recompense.

* * * *

The only assistance father had in attending to the garden, apart from our inexperienced help, was from his brother. Our help consisted mainly of collecting the scores of small branches father had pruned off the fruit trees. Having assisted to this degree we may have felt justified in taking our unofficial share of the Victoria plums which always seemed to be in heavy branched profusion. Our difficulty was disposing of the stones in a non tell-tale position. We had similar difficulties with the pea pod shells when they were in season.

But the highlight of father's garden season was the Potato Growing Competition. This was organised by the Allotments Association of which my father was a member. The competition was for the heaviest crop from fourteen sets. The variety was kept secret until after the results were known and the sets were planted under the supervision of committee members. Times without number the competition was won by my father and, I think, his record weight for the fourteen sets was 282 lbs. No one, other than himself, knew the secret of his success but many wished that they could share that secret. He may have been lucky enough to drop on some suitable fertiliser or something which suited the particular soil in our garden but, whenever asked about it, he always claimed it was something 'out of his waistcoat pocket' and this became quite a catch phrase to allotment members. He reserved quite a considerable area for his crop and it had to be admitted the growth and the size of the haulms were really exceptional.

The lifting of everybody's crop occupied the whole of an autumn Saturday as each contestant was visited in turn with Committee members present to see fair play. The oohs and the aahs as each root was lifted was interposed with some jocular comment as a poor root was unearthed. Finally, in a sack, the whole crop was weighed on a large spring balance suspended by a stout pole across the shoulders of the stronger two of the company. "Well done Sam" they would murmur, some grudgingly, as an unassailable weight was announced. But they all knew full well that up at the house there would be beer all round. My father had the good sense of fair play to ensure that the beer appeared after the lifting and not before. He would collect his prize at the next Allotment Flower Show but, knowing father, the prize money would be given back into the funds. No doubt he would also have won a prize for his gladioli which he had tended with such care through the summer. Curiously enough he also entered for the table decoration class and I am sure his artistic eye ensured that his entry was tastefully done. He always claimed that the entries of his opponents were "too heavy". It was not quite clear in our minds what exactly he had in mind, and this expression, too, became something of a catch phrase at home. When Ena entered the field in this class we all whispered to her to ensure she didn't make her entry "too heavy".

This show, held in the Guildhall, was looked forward to each year. The produce and the flowers in all the various classes were voluminous. Colonel Swinfen Broun, a patron and originator of the concept, always sent his head gardener along from Swinfen Hall, with a massive collection of blooms and vegetables which were gathered into a huge display but, of course, were not allowed to be entered for competition. The event was always well attended and gardening enthusiasts thronged between the laden rows on display. On any other day, when the steps up to the Guildhall were climbed, there was a distinct aroma of Mansion Polish from the dance floor but during the show this was replaced by the stronger smell of garden vegetables and the scent of blooms which even pervaded down into Bore Street below.

There was always great fun and banter at the conclusion of the evening when, after the prize distribution and speeches, the head of a local firm of auctioneers stepped forward to sell all the accumulated produce. He was affectionately known in the City as 'Blinker' because of the way he screwed up his face in a succession of blinks and nods when talking or looking for further bids. Then, when the hall had been cleared, my father would bring the other members of the Committee home and around the table, well supplied

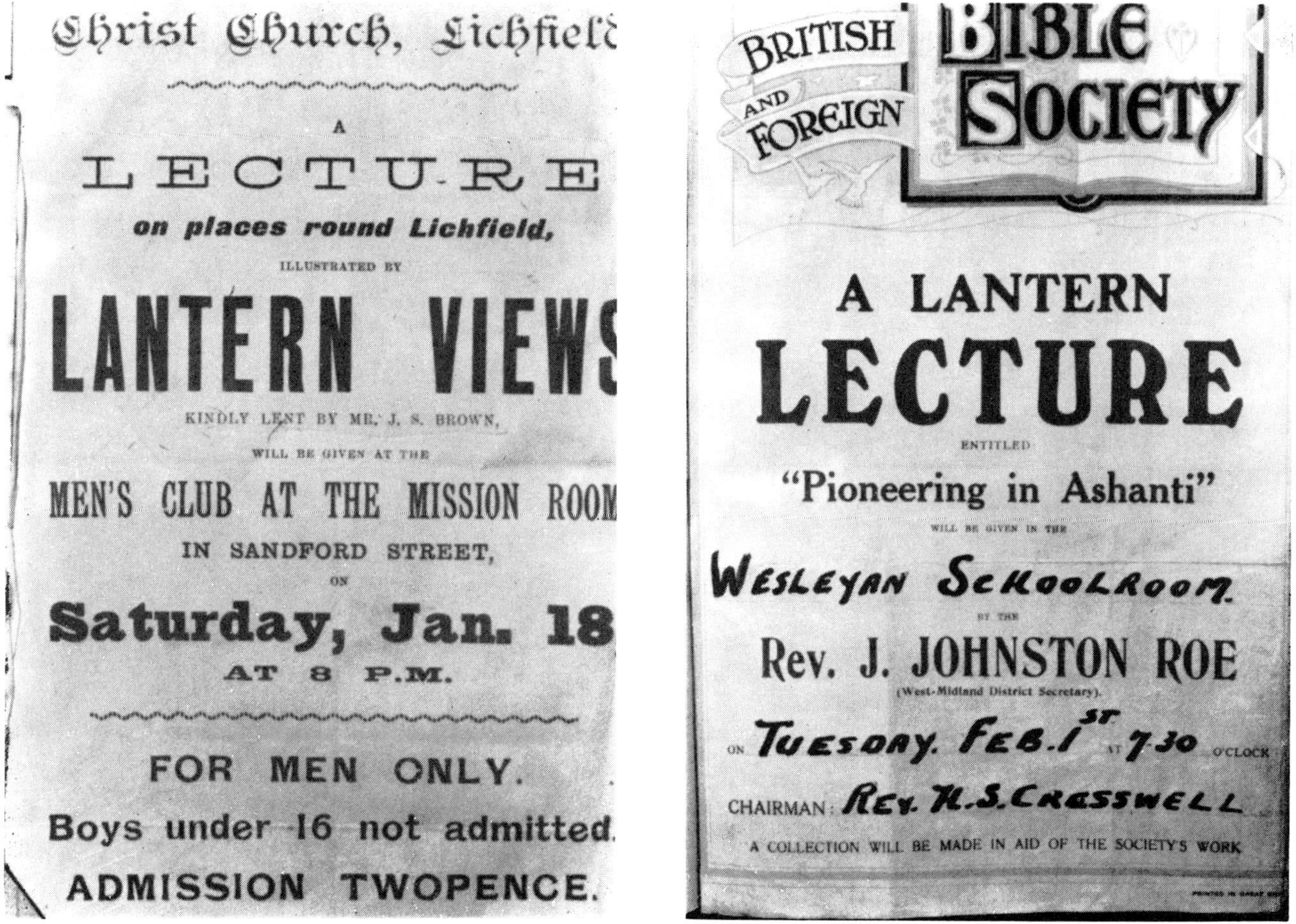

Christ Church, Lichfield

A

LECTURE

on places round Lichfield,

ILLUSTRATED BY

LANTERN VIEWS

KINDLY LENT BY MR. J. S. BROWN,

WILL BE GIVEN AT THE

MEN'S CLUB AT THE MISSION ROOM

IN SANDFORD STREET,

ON

Saturday, Jan. 18

AT 8 P.M.

FOR MEN ONLY.

Boys under 16 not admitted.

ADMISSION TWOPENCE.

BRITISH AND FOREIGN BIBLE SOCIETY

A LANTERN

LECTURE

ENTITLED

"Pioneering in Ashanti"

WILL BE GIVEN IN THE

WESLEYAN SCHOOLROOM.

BY THE

Rev. J. JOHNSTON ROE

(West-Midland District Secretary).

ON TUESDAY. FEB. 1ST AT 7.30 O'CLOCK

CHAIRMAN: REV. H. S. CRESSWELL

A COLLECTION WILL BE MADE IN AID OF THE SOCIETY'S WORK

Lantern Lecture Notices

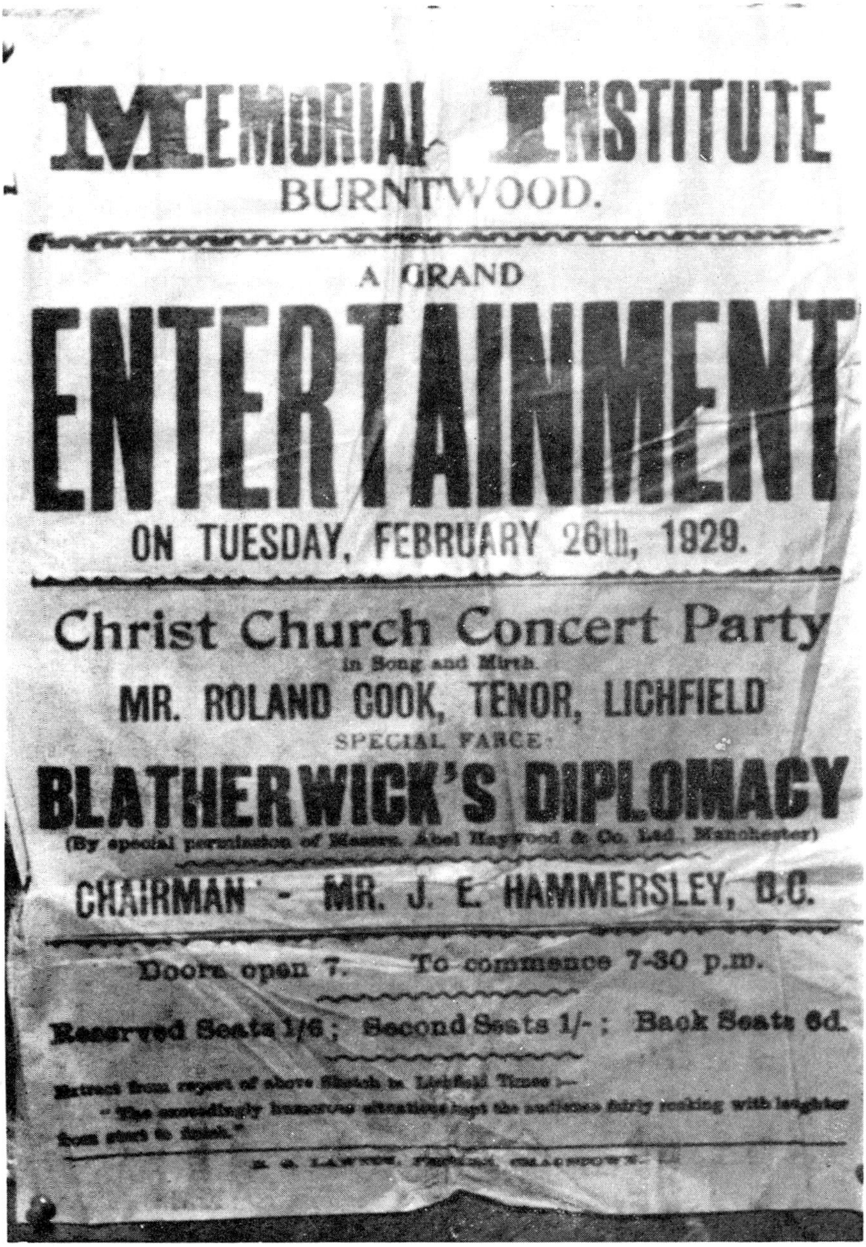

MEMORIAL INSTITUTE
BURNTWOOD.

A GRAND
ENTERTAINMENT
ON TUESDAY, FEBRUARY 26th, 1929.

Christ Church Concert Party
in Song and Mirth
MR. ROLAND COOK, TENOR, LICHFIELD
SPECIAL FARCE:
BLATHERWICK'S DIPLOMACY
(By special permission of Messrs. Abel Haywood & Co. Ltd., Manchester)

CHAIRMAN - MR. J. E. HAMMERSLEY, O.C.

Doors open 7. To commence 7-30 p.m.

Reserved Seats 1/6; Second Seats 1/-; Back Seats 6d.

Extract from report of above Sketch in Lichfield Times :—
"The exceedingly humorous situations kept the audience fairly rocking with laughter from start to finish."

Christ Church Concert Party Notice

with father's beer, they would sit talking through the events of the day just gone. Holding his glass up to the light, one silver haired stalwart with a red outdoor face, which matched his button hole, wiping the froth from his moustache and then looking to the others and winking, would say "a bit of good stuff in this Sam!" and they'd all laugh, knowing his reference also applied to the secret ingredients Sam put under his potatoes from his waistcoat pocket.

* * * *

My father was a keen photographer and there can be few families who have been photographed so often and so consistently. We have many albums which not only depict us in progressive ages but also bears witness to the fact that he was taking photographs before even the turn of the century. Photographs are a wonderful reminder of days gone by and yet, many of the fading prints show faces and figures of past friends and family members who, unfortunately, we are now unable to identify. Our experiences of being photographed are very similar to sketches and parodies of such occasions. It did seem an age for him to set up the cumbersome plate camera and adjust it on the tripod with his head eveloped under a red velvet cover. It was at this stage that we could break out into giggles which would continue in a suppressed way until adjusted into the smiles he would eventually call for.

But as is the case with most hobbies they progress and improve and to this end father procured a "magic lantern" with which to show the results of his work in addition to the albums. He developed all his prints and set about transferring the negatives on to projection slides. The lantern itself progressed through different stages from the original acetylene lime light to transformer and finally mains electric lighting.

Having in mind there was no television and little radio and cinemas were in their early days, the lantern became most popular and he gave shows to varying audiences. Gradually lecturers came along with slides to illustrate their talks and as his was one of the few lanterns available he found himself in much demand. I attended many such lectures over the years, mainly to run and carry all the odds and ends of equipment and, I am ashamed to admit, I joined the spontaneous laughter with which a slide projected upside down was always received. But I always felt such laughter was a sure sign that some of the audience were becoming a little restive and the errors came as a light relief. It also amused me to listen for the little 'click' indicator which the lecturer held in his hand and pressed when he wished the next slide to be shown. This sometimes led to a slight panic in my mind when I thought father had missed hearing one of the click-clicks but my fears were soon allayed, as several clicks in succession always quickly followed.

In those days the screen could be a problem, for the spring loaded modern variety were, obviously, not available. They were usually linen sheets with tapes sewn at intervals along the edge and tied to a bamboo frame to achieve tautness. But if a sheet is stored without care for any length of time the resulting creases mar the picture. Because of this mother had, frequently, to provide one of her best carefully ironed household sheets at the last moment.

Many of the lectures and slide shows related to church matters including the Nativity at Christmas. We also had a regular arrangement for the 'Story of the Cross' on Good Friday at the village church of Wall just outside Lichfield. I see my father now, high up over and with one foot on, the altar in some difficulty finding a niche on which to secure the bamboo frame. My brother and myself would, ourselves, be scrambling over the choir stalls in an attempt to attain stability of the swaying structure. The whole thing has been known to collapse, yet I am sure any slight oath emitted from father, in a position now near the pipes of the organ, would be forgiven having in mind the object of the exercise. The Vicar, the Reverend Ashworth had the most angelic and Christian countenance with silver hair and at the end of the service, in his best manner, he would nod at us and thank father for coming along and taking so much trouble to help ensure a rewarding evening and added that the slides had added much reverence and meaning to the service. As we turned to collect and pack up the equipment I am sure father gave us a smile and a wink.

* * * *

Between the wars it was usual for parish churches to arrange parochial teas and entertainments near Christmas or the New Year. These teas were usually funded by a system of subscriptions called 'trays'. Five shillings for a full tray and half a crown for a half tray. My father had been in the choir of the local Christ Church since he was a boy and it was this senior position which allowed him, along with the choirmaster, to organise the entertainment part of the evening. The partitions of all four classrooms of the nearby school would be rolled back and tea table after tea table stretched across the opened expanse. Eventually, after the meal, the tables were cleared and the participants turned and rearranged their chairs to face the stage.

The concert, always of local people, consisted of about twelve acts which led up to a final play or, more usually, a farce. This always had the audience rocking with laughter, the more so because they knew those taking part. My father and a fellow choirman with a walrus moustache always took the comic parts. I recall one such production called 'Blatherwick's Diplomacy' and I see my father poking his head over the back screen to look down on some severe over acting of an embarrasing but harmless situation below. Care would be taken not to go too far as this was, after all, a church gathering. Having assembled such a 'Bill of Fare' and with the concerts becoming so widely known and popular, other churches and outlying villages invited the company along to repeat the show for them.

How simple and pleasant were these occasions with the audiences so appreciative of local talent, the old songs and good honest voices. The soprano, a relation of ours, rose high above the chorus in her rendering of 'Somewhere a voice is calling' and tears were hard to hold back as another parishioner gave her annual, yet always welcome, offering of 'Danny Boy'.

For more special occasions to bolster this modest talent one of the tenors from the Cathedral choir was drawn in and who usually sang and asked in rich tones 'Who is Sylvia?'. He was Roland Cook and father was able to persuade him to join the company because he knew him well as wicketkeeper

St. John Street and Bore Street Corner

Bore Street Corner

for the Lichfield First Eleven. Another relative, Alf Bull, who had fought as an officer on the Somme could not forsake his military bearing as he stood bolt upright to recite 'The Green Eye of the little Yellow God' in a piping voice that belied his association with commands on the Barrack Square. Then there was the local ventriloquist, Alfred Cope, whom my brother and myself watched intently from the side wings, as we suspected we could see his lips moving. His patter, today, would perhaps be termed corny. Asked to repeat 'The murderer lay on his truckle bed' the dummy replied 'The murderer lay on a coal truck'. But we all laughed and enjoyed it.

I never took part in any of these productions but, with Dennis, travelled around with the company and helped off stage with the props. My elder brother, John, joined in and complete with dog collar and flat black hat recited 'The Parsons of Puddle' and later, with Ena, sang the duet 'O Sarah — O 'enery'. Father would come in with a song called 'Riddles' and, with the organist, render 'Mr. Gallagher and Mr. Shean'. The whole evening was interposed with enthusiastic yet controlled and dignified rounds of applause.

How happy and free were our minds as we turned out from those village halls on winter nights into the fresh smelling air of the countryside and when our only concern was whether to risk cycling home without lighting up!

* * * *

In addition to the winter concerts father also organised outings in the summer for those who were not so well off and were, perhaps, confined to a life in institutions. They all loved him for it and would look forward to the event from one years end to the other. He arranged a fleet of cars to transport them on a wide circular tour around the outskirts of Lichfield including the Milford Hills and Cannock Chase. The tour would finish up at Hopwas Woods between Lichfield and Tamworth. On arrival at the woods long rows of table-clothed trestle tables were set out and heaped with appropriate food. It has to be admitted that sandwiches to the fore would not necessarily have graced the tea tables on the vicarage lawn, yet they all quickly disappeared. A large tea urn with a huge brass tap stood at the head of each table and enamel tea pots enabled the many helpers to transfer the steaming brew into the waiting line of white mugs.

These men and women were in a new world here, free and far away from the dark green and brown drabness of the walls of the rooms then inhabited for the rest of the year. Many suffered some physical and mental handicap yet, as I saw them, their faces had broad smiles, they were happy out there and they were willing to join in the games and dancing arranged amongst the sun dappled clearing in the wood. And then, finally, they all joined in with, perhaps, unharmonious voices, the community singing with all the old songs led only by the cornet player of the City Band. Even then the more versatile would insist in dancing a jig to the music.

Then a final, unrehearsed ritual was always enacted, although each year it came as a surprise. One of the regular volunteers would step forward from the confines of the committee tent where he had been reinforcing his resolve with the more potent beverage reserved for the helpers. Under a heavy moustache he would step forward and strike up, unaccompanied, the familiar strains of "The End of a Perfect Day". Hesitant in getting into his swing and so indistinct were his words, we wondered if he had got hold of the right song. But gradually, with the help of the cornet player, who had now recognised and picked up the tune, he got going and in the gathering summer dusk everyone joined in and carried the old song into a second and third verse.

Eventually a worried Sam "felt he must get them back" and they were all persuaded to return to the waiting cars for rather a sad journey. But, without fail, practically the whole of the company would approach my father and say a heartfelt "thank you".

* * * *

My father was always thinking of ways and means of raising funds for the local hospital. In the early twenties he had one such idea in the form of a Grand Penny Race between the Clock Tower, then standing at the head of Bore Street, and the hospital itself, situated some 200 yards away in Sandford Street. Double white lines were to be painted along the centre of the footpaths and father challenged a local business friend, Mr. W. H. Bolton whose shop, the Bolton Warehouse Co., was situated on the route in Bird Street, as to who could reach the hospital first with pennies cajoled or otherwise from the passers by and placed on the selected white line.

The race was held on a Friday, market day, when the town was reasonably full with the influx of the farming communities from outside. It had a unique appeal and went like wild fire early in the morning with the lines of pennies quickly extending along Bird Street in the direction of Sandford Street and the hospital some way along. For hours the contestants ran neck and neck and there was much joviality amongst the continual knot of spectators. Friends of one or the other came along with a larger bulk of pennies and as one surged slightly ahead a cheer would be raised. During the lunch hour the flow of coins wained. Helpers gathered up the rear guard of pennies into their blue bank bags ready for counting. I always suspected, probably quite wrongly, some of those rear guard pennies were discreetly re-introduced after lunch to whip up further enthusiasm. In any case the race was given quite a boost during the afternoon because before tea time the line had turned Sandford Street corner and was pressing well on for the hospital. My brother and I were highly delighted because father had taken quite a lead. About this time, I learned later, one of my father's business friends came along with a huge bag of coppers and could have settled the outcome of the race there and then. He said to father "where will you have them Sam?". Now I am sure had the question been addressed to me I would have quickly boosted father's line and, indeed, father may well have had an inclination to do the same but, to his credit, he advised his friend to place them on his adversaries line "to help make a race of it". From then on until dusk the race proceeded neck and neck. But, alas, there was not to be a finish in a blaze of glory for, with it getting quite dark, the race had to be abandoned with honours even and the pennies some yards short of the goal.

I have said that both the Clock Tower and Hospital held prominent positions

The Clock Tower at time of transfer

The new position, Friary Road (in Moggs area)

The Victoria Cottage Hospital

Swinfen Hall, seat of Lichfield benefactor, Colonel M. A. Swinfen Broun

in the town. The former especially so. It dominated the junction of Bore Street and Bird Street and was built so near to the edge of the pavement that it formed quite a traffic bottleneck. It was an imposing structure and the populace were much endeared to it. It had been erected about 1860 after a street clock, in Breadmarket Street, had been taken down and some bright spark had seen the plans for London's Big Ben Tower and thought Lichfield should have one as well. But many people wanted the clock near the Guildhall or Dr. Johnson's birthplace and there was considerable objection. Eventually it was built on land owned by the Conduit Land's Trust who paid the cost of £1,200. It had difficulties throughout its life time not the least of which were its illumination at night and the accuracy of its time keeping. At one stage someone had to walk down to Trent Valley Station each day to obtain the correct London time from the guard on the 10 a.m. train from Euston. He then trailed back and adjusted the hands. However, in 1925, the City and County Councils of the day made the brave decision to move it lock, stock and barrel, to a new position several hundred yards away to the south west and incorporate the site in a new road system which was designed, apart from taking the danger away from Bore Street corner, to give relief to Birmingham Road, Walsall Road, St. John Street and Bird Street. The decision to remove it met with just as strong objections as those first raised on its erection. 'Lichfield would never be the same again' it was said. But moved the tower was and, with time, the revised position has become accepted and has matured to remain a feature of the present town.

The traffic at Bore Street junction was always controlled by a policeman on point duty and even when the new crossroad was formed he was retained. He was a well known and well liked character who gave his signals in a most precise manner with an exaggerated flick of the wrist and a white gloved finger pointed dramatically in the direction he thought you wanted to go. He had a pleasant smiling face and for this reason everyone called him 'panshine'. Even when he was finally superseded by traffic signals the installation took over his control point in the centre of the road and the four faces of the lights operated there from on one heavy base. But not only was the Clock Tower, the starting point of the Penny Race, removed and transferred, so also was the finishing point of the race — the Hospital.

This Hospital, or Nursing Home as it was more usually called, in Sandford Street was a former private residence adapted for medical and surgical uses and had served local needs very well over a long period of time under difficulties. Only a few years previously my sister had undergone an operation here for the removal of her adenoids and tonsils which was not, perhaps, the straight forward operation it would be today. I remember being in the street below, with my mother, looking up at the hospital windows and wondering how she was going on. Suffice to say no one need have worried because Ena came round from the anaesthetic satisfactorily and her only concern had been the noise kicked up in the street below by a steamroller scarifying the road surface.

But the hospital was in need of more space and better facilities and to replace it The Victoria Cottage Hospital was built within a stone's throw of its counterpart in the Penny Race and took advantage of the fine new wide verged roads leading up to it. There were many other money raising schemes to achieve the final amount and I remember joining in with other school children in taking money to school to buy a brick for the building. Eventually, on Empire Day,

May 24, 1932, the Foundation Stone was laid by Mrs. M. A. Swinfen Broun.

But reverting back to the Penny Race it has never occurred to me, until this moment, to wonder how many pennies were involved and a quick calculation suggests there would be, in the two rows, some 12,000. Having in mind the time and effort spent on this project the £50 by which the hospital benefitted seems, by the values of today, meagre indeed.

* * * *

I have omitted to add that my father was, in his spare time, a keen amateur conjuror. His performances were restricted to the drawing rooms and family parties. Here the eyes were closer and all around him which gave him less margin of error and the sleight-of-hand more difficult. We had the advantage of knowing the drawer where he kept all this tricks and were thus able to fathom out and solve all the mysteries. Eventually we were drawn in to help him by setting up his props in the background. When asked for an encore he, very wisely, claimed that "a conjuror never did the same trick twice". On his frequent visits to London he made a point of calling in at Gamages to buy new tricks and, if he had time, visited a performance at the Maskeylene and Cook Theatre.

* * * *

At my father's parting service a prebendary of the Cathedral addressed an overflowing church at St. Chad's and gave thanks for an extraordinary life of service and help to the community and referred to father as a universal secretary. This Churchman also allowed himself to express the view that Sam, even in Heaven, might well help with the administration.

But for myself, my mind went back to summer evenings at home of long ago, hauling the mower up and down the tennis lawn, father pushing hard whilst my brothers and myself struggled with the rope tied to the front of the grassbox — to father meeting us off a train with an anxious face turning to pleasure as he saw us alight — to days in the sunshine with him on the cricket field — to hear him every morning, whilst shaving, practising intonations of the psalms in his high pitched alto voice — all the happy times we shared and be home again in time for supper altogether. At that service I learned, for the first time, how final death was and I knew, then, that we had lost our best friend.

Chapter Five

MY MOTHER

My mother was, to me, a perfect gentle woman. Kind, caring, completely unselfish and considerate of others, well dressed; she set a wonderful example to all of us.

She had strongly held principles of social behaviour and she may well have appeared, at times, to be straight-laced. Yet to those who knew her best she was so easy to get on with, amusing in conversation with a sense of humour. This was a humour of her own, nurtured when a girl amongst brothers and sisters, which she adjusted to the livelier, perhaps more impish good fun, in the happy home she was moulding with my father. The sound of laughter rang through and permeated into the very rooms themselves, to mealtimes, yet subdued and controlled to conform to table behaviour, and echoed in from across the tennis lawn outside. The house became alive, with mother smiling a welcome as we came in, the tea pot at hand for the unexpected caller or a greeting to our many school friends passing through. Always a look back and a wave from the gate and pleasure as footsteps returned along to the door at the side of the house. She took a positive stance in most things and was always optimistic and cheerful.

In our illnesses, having administered medicine considered appropriate, she would settle us down for the night, probably rubbing menthol on our foreheads, with the words "You'll be better in the morning". She has, indeed, been able to convince us that a sore throat could be cured by eating merely a boiled egg. Although the story is told that when Dennis appeared not to be eating very well and in a quantity sufficient to satisfy mother she consulted the family doctor.

"Where is he now Mrs. Brown?" he asked.

"Oh, he is out playing football with his brothers."

"Then there is not much the matter with him." the doctor answered. "I think I would not worry anymore about it."

At this time there was a fashion to own an autograph book. The books were usually quite small with leaves of varying colours bound in an attractive cover. They were not used for collecting the signatures of the famous but for family or friends to enter a drawing or write an anecdote, poem or quotation — in fact, an offering of ones own choice. My mother entered the following verse in mine back in 1927: it spoke for the philosophy of her life —

"Speak kindly, oh, speak kindly,
You little know the worth
Of words of loving kindness
As you travel thro' this earth."

Often as boys we may have been working up to a quarrel and she would quell it by quoting the first line — "Speak kindly, oh, speak kindly" and more often than not her words would have the desired effect and normal brotherly relations would be restored.

She lived in the same street in Lichfield all her life. First in the bakers shop near the top of the hill at the corner of Greenhough Row and later, in successive moves after she was married. She spoke often of the graciousness of the period in which she had been brought up, one of a large family of eight children. How she lost her mother when she was eighteen and then afterwards her father, the loss of whom meant, although there were still four brothers, the breaking up of the bakery business in which they had all been involved.

It is not surprising that she told many stories about this business. Of the man who came into the shop occasionally, pressed his thumb into a currant bun from a pile displayed on the counter saying, "How much for the damaged one missus?", and how a hot cross bun was nailed, each year, to a beam in the bakehouse and there it remained until the next Easter, the mix being so good that it came to no harm. Another story she related concerned a contract the company had won for the daily supply of bread to the military barracks at Whittington, just outside the city. A high horse drawn two wheeled cart with a framed canvas hood would, each day, make the four mile journey stacked high with loaves. When the rear curtains of the hood were drawn aside row upon row of loaves could be seen in all their crusty golden glory.

On this occasion a rather superior type of subaltern, probably just commissioned, appeared from his quarters to receive the bread. In a high handed manner he ordered the curtains to be parted and immediately, with little examination, rejected the load, instructing that the bread be taken back. To his surprise the two brothers in charge of the load turned the cart round and without demur set off back in the direction of Lichfield. But they pulled up in the yard of the Horse and Jockey Inn some little distance along the road, took out the rear rows of loaves and replaced them with bread from the front rows. They had a drink at the inn, hung about for a while then, with some ceremony, returned to the barracks. Touching their caps to the same officer they again opened the curtains and the officer said "Ah, that's better, thank you, wonderful bread, wonderful load of bread".

My mother went to school in Lichfield at a small private academy further down the street in the direction of the town at Dimble House and she was very proud of the establishment and stayed on to help with the teaching. There could not have been many pupils but she received a splendid education and often quoted Miss Yeend whose school it was. Emphasis was made in the teaching of the Bible which she came to know thoroughly. English literature was also a favourite subject and she frequently referred to passages from the classic books and quoted from poems to illustrate a particular aspect of life. Chief of her poems was, by far, the 'Deserted Village' and she was always quoting from it. She loved the passages involving the village Schoolmaster and the Preacher "passing rich with forty pounds a year" and wondered, with Goldsmith, "how one small head could carry all he knew". She frequently mentioned, too, those who came to church "to scoff but remain'd to pray".

She had a secure faith, taught to her by her mother and reinforced by the guidance of Miss Yeend. This background was deeply rooted in her mind which, no doubt, had a wide influence in her life and the manner in which she brought up her family She would kneel each Sunday morning in her bedroom beneath the picture of Holman Hunt's 'Light of the World' on the

Mother with the inevitable knitting

Dennis and myself in our unlined blue suits

The Hygienic Bakery, Beacon Street

The Bread Cart at George's Baker Shop
(corner Beacon Street and Greenhough Row)

Holman Hunt's 'Light of the World'

St. Chad's Church

St. John's Hospital and St. John's Church

wall near her dressing table and say, for she knew them all by heart, the Collect for the Day followed by the Lord's Prayer and, if we were with her, we would join in and follow her words. In her early years, just before and immediately after her marriage, she always attended a small and less known church in the city, St. John's — the church to which Miss Yeend had introduced her. She took Ena and John to Evensong before Dennis and myself were born. She loved those intimate little services and told us of the vicar's five minute sermons, a deep and simple text, delivered as if over tea in a drawing room, yet from the heart rather than from written notes. "Truth from his lips prevail'd with double sway"! Even the hymns were introduced with a sense of ownership and nostalgia. "And now another of our favourite hymns, ancient and modern number 176 — 'How sweet the name of Jesus sounds in a believer's ear.' Isn't it far better to sing the hymns we all know and enjoy rather than those through which we struggle". The present day hymns and tunes and certainly the alternate prayer book would hardly have been acceptable to those at St. John's.

As we grew older she attended St. Chad's, her own parish church more and took all her children with her. Curiously my father did not always go with us. He had been a member of the choir since his youth at Christ Church, and had continued singing there after his marriage. We did go to this church on occasions and it was strange to see him in his white surplus, processing in the choir. He seemed so serious, so remote and so different from the smiling intimate father we knew at home. Mother tended not to go to this church too often because, I suspect, she did not like sitting away from him; he in the choir stalls, she amidst the congregation. Even when father came with us to morning service he would attend his own evensong and would set off across the field path in his dark suit, bowler hat and silver knobbed cherry walking stick and we would hear the five minutes bell start as he disappeared, a hurrying figure, into the distance.

Of the two churches I liked mother's the better, mainly, I think, because there were more diversions to attract our rather unholy attention. The grown ups in the choir were all known to us and we saw them about Lichfield often, and it caused us some amusement to have to recognise them in their unfamiliar church garb and with strange facial contortions in their efforts to keep pace and to be heard against the thunderings of the organ.

I also recall this church with some discomfort for the very reason that the pews were always so cold, which to small boys in short blue suit trousers was not conducive to sitting through, let alone listening to, a sermon. On one occasion we were wearing new suits for the first time. Trousers, in those days, were usually made with a reasonably warm lining, but for some reason linings had been omitted from these particular pairs and, whilst willing to give them a trial, we were quickly made aware of the tailor's error when we made contact with the pew. Mother accepted the subsequent complaint and the trousers were returned for amendment. Whilst on the subject of boys' trousers I can think of nothing more painful than wearing a pair whose rough lower edges rubbed and chaffed the leg just above the knee. We would turn them up to obtain relief but then the white lining would be exposed. The afflicted areas, especially on a cold day, quickly became very red and fierce and mother would have to bathe them with Boracic powder. I suspect this Boracic powder cured quite a number of our ills.

The services I liked most of all at this church were the Harvest Festivals. Even the Mayor and Corporation attended in procession and with much pomp led by the City Band. The band accompanied most such occasions. It pleased us to hear the thump of the band as it approached unseen, along Stowe Street from the direction of the city and then, as it swung into view round the corner by Stowe Pool tootling and blaring away at "Sons of the Brave". We just had time to join mother in our pew at the back of the church before the solemn official party entered, all with dignified and appropriate Sunday faces.

Even at that age we loved the Harvest hymns and sang them with some gusto. But these hymns at St. Chad's were reinforced by a trumpeter from the band who swung high into a pleasant descant on some of the verses. The band master also joined in as he produced his violin, deposited previously under the pulpit, and added his contribution to increase the mellowness of the familiar tunes.

The church would always be fully loaded with sheaves of corn, bright red apples and other fruit, with all sorts of highly scrubbed vegetables dominated by huge marrows. The farmers in the area generously contributed vast amounts of produce and, with allotment holders and gardeners adding their share, the surrounds of the lectern and pulpit stacked high, offered ample testimony that all had been safely gathered in. On the Monday following, all would be transferred to the adjacent school rooms where, in the evening, my father and an uncle would auction it all off in a jocular rather than a professional manner. Bidders were not run up, unless they were a local dignatory, or pressed to extend their bid, but church funds nevertheless benefitted very considerably and many parishioners struggled home with unexpected and heavy bargains of high quality.

Although mother took us to church regularly from a young age it was some time before we became aware of the inner and deeper meaning of the faith. At Christmas, for instance, after we had been up with our stockings since about half past five, mother and father, and later Ena and John, would disappear for an hour or so at about 7.30. It never occurred to us to wonder, or even ask, where they were going, mainly because we were still concentrating on the business of going through our stockings and reaching the orange, the apple and the chocolate coins in the toe. Eventually, of course, we set off with them. We had by then attended Sunday School and had been confirmed in the Cathedral.

My family only attended services in the Cathedral on special occasions but we were, nevertheless, very conscious of having such a magnificent building — and mother church of the diocese — within our town. Mother instilled into us that it was the smallest yet the most lovely of all Cathedrals. She made us fully aware of the beauty of the Spires, the hundred and more statues of kings, apostles and saints on the west front and, inside, the statue of the sleeping children. We knew every exquisite detail of this gem — the lifelike little feet and the fingers clasping the snowdrops — because father had a lantern slide of it and, as we studied it on the screen he would tell of the tragedy of the two little girls and their parents.

Although the Cathedral was so familiar to us and we saw it every day there was always a sense of strangeness and awe whenever we stepped inside. We knew well the various clergy and the vergers and members of the Vicar's Choral in the everyday life of the City. One of them played cricket with us and

The Cathedral, taken from the Dam Street end of Pool Walk

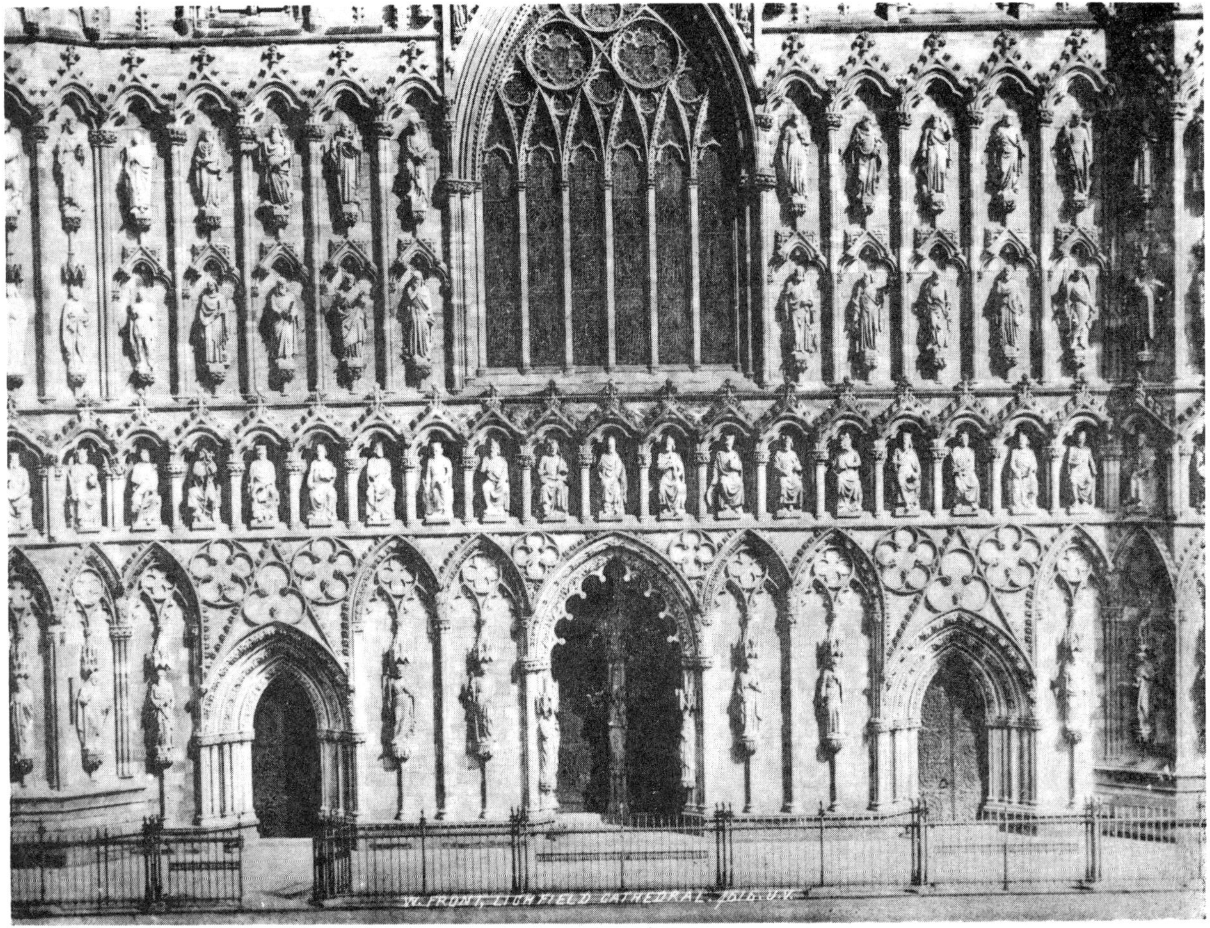

The glory of the West Front

The grandeur of the Cathedral interior

The Sleeping Children

frequently, during a Saturday afternoon home match, he left the game for an hour to attend and sing at Evensong. We often wondered how many times his mind wandered from the psalms to the wickets falling half a mile away on the cricket field.

The very presence of the Cathedral in our lives gave a feeling of pride and respect and when we walked about the precincts, through the Close and along the tree lined Dean's Walk round into Dam Street an unfailing atmosphere of strength and solemnity pervaded. This same feeling filtered inside to the high vaulted ceilings and the grandeur, as we looked eastward down the whole length of the nave, past the choir stalls through to the High Altar. Amidst all this the organist of that time, Ambrose Porter, produced his unforgettable quality of music which flowed and swirled around us and often culminated in a crescendo of sound to a degree that we felt even the Cathedral itself was trembling.

It was amidst this atmosphere and with these feelings of awe, respect and reverence when on an April day in 1931, during an impressive confirmation service, I found myself at the side of Dennis advancing slowly towards the Bishop Kempthorne, a commanding figure in full regalia, to kneel together to receive his blessing and laying on of hands.

As mother moved into older age we noticed that, whilst obviously not losing her faith, she tended not to wish to go down to church so often. We did not look for nor ask for any specific reason but I have little doubt that changes in outlook in the ministry and procedures were rather alien to the traditions she had been taught and known since she was a girl and which she had held in strong belief all that time. I know, too, how deeply offended she and other parishioners had been when, with little or no reference to them, their well loved Saint Chad's Well was destroyed and a modern counterpart substituted some distance away, they said, from the genuine spot.

* * * *

Discipline in our home was firm but not severe and neither parent ever hit us in any way. I think we were made to feel rather ashamed of ourselves for the transgressions into which we had fallen. Once, for instance, we must have made an awful mess in the bathroom when we had been sent up to get ready for a visit to the local Shrove Tuesday Fair. Water was over the floor, sponges thrown about, towels awry and soap nowhere to be seen. This was, perhaps, the only occasion I saw my mother more than angry. We realised it was so unfair on her, not only to have to face the mess, but that it was all caused by an outing arranged for us and one which she would not have taken for herself alone. Rightly the outing was cancelled and we were exiled, for the time being, to our room where we had plenty of time to feel sorry for ourselves and, at the same time, I hope, feel sorry for mother. But she was probably feeling just as unhappy as we were, would relent and come up to our room with some tea. We would say we were sorry but that didn't mean we were free to leave the bedroom for we had to stay on.

Usually, though, mother made sure we were not still up there by the time father came home. There was no need, however, for her to protect us from him for quite often he had to deal with our misdeeds or accidents himself. The kitchen window may well have been broken by a misdirected tennis ball, or a football had landed in a flower bed, cutting off precious blooms. With guilt all over our faces we would stand there holding in our hands the pathetic broken head of a chrysanthemum. We also played football in the house, sometimes heading ballons with the door as a goal. At that time the house was lit by gas and entailed the use of gas mantles, which on burning were hopelessly brittle and fragile and the least knock would cause them to collapse. On one occasion such a catastrophe occurred as the balloon soared up and, as there were no replacements in the cupboard, mother sent us down to the street emporium to buy one, thinking that all would be well before father arrived home. But even best laid plans can fail for who should be in very shop but father and we had to blurt out we had broken the mantle and had come for a new one.

* * * *

Beneath a strong will and a certain proudness, mother was very soft-hearted. We had our problems and little troubles which she helped to solve but not necessarily always in our favour. I am sure she also had her own heartaches, many of them quite unknown to us, but in our need she was always there, comforting and helpful. Incidents occurred which, at the time, were exaggerated into tragedies out of all proportion to their real significance and tears would be shed. Examples come to mind.

When our boots wore out mother usually called in at Frisby's, near the Market Square, and arranged with Mr. Horton, the manager, to send up a new selection from which to choose. We would see the errand boy arrive and eagerly rushed into the kitchen where mother had already set them out in a row. The selection varied in style, some of which were quite sturdy — they had to be for our usage. Mother allowed us to inspect them to see which we would like and we set about our detailed assessment. We quickly and unanimously decided we wanted the ones called "Little Dukes". The name was embroidered on the label tag above the heel and furthermore, and it was this which attracted us to them, the three top positions for the laces were not holes but tags on which the lace had to be hooked. They were really superior looking boots in our eyes, but I have no doubt they were the most expensive by far and the tags, mother explained, would soon break off and be useless. We pressed hard for the Little Dukes but despite our tears we lost the day and mother bought the more serviceable and less expensive pairs.

My first football boots were also the cause of tears. A lovely pair were purchased for me and they were my pride and joy and, although the grass was very wet, I tried them out on the tennis lawn. Trying to get them dry I placed them on the kitchen fire hob with the soles and studs near to, and facing, the embers. There I left them drying but, unfortunately, I forget them. When I chanced to pass by later I found, to my horror, the soles burnt and shrivelled up and quite ruined. Full of tears I took them to mother and held them up pathetically. Mother came up trumps "Never mind Cuth" she said consolingly, "we will have to get another pair".

But mother shed tears as well, both of joy and sadness. The first occasion I saw tears happened when my brother and myself had gone off after tea to the canal for skating. It had been a hard spell of frost and we felt satisfied the ice was safe even though the weight was considerable with many of our school friends gathering there. To add to mother's apprehension it was quite dark before we returned home and on seeing us back safely she could not suppress tears of relief. I realised, then, the anxiety of waiting at home for loved ones and I have known it myself, many times, when I too, became a parent.

I also saw my mother's tears many years later but in a sequence that must have happened in many families the world over. My sister married in 1935 and she left home with her husband for him to continue his career in far away China. This, to mother who had lived not only in the same town but the same street all her life, was something of a wrench. She had, no doubt, dreamed a dream that one day grandchildren would climb to her knee there in her own home. Even Ena, happy to be with her husband though she was, may have looked out from her window across the teeming, dry, foreign Chinese landscape and dreamed a dream herself of the "cooling brook, the grassy vested green" back at home. But eventually the letter mother knew would come arrived; a grandchild was on the way.

Some few days later I found mother alone in her bedroom. I sat on the edge of the bed facing the window where I could see out to the fields and where in a few minutes I would be setting off with my dog. She mentioned Ena and said to me "I wish I could be with her". I daresay I made some clumsy attempt to solace her. I knew she had been rummaging in the front of the drawer of her dressing table and had pulled out a bunch of old papers secured loosely with a green tape and, glancing through them, said she was posting them on to China. There were tears in her eyes. Apparently the papers were of advice and help which she had used thirty years ago when she, herself, had had Ena. And now, just when she thought they would be read and used again by her own daughter, she was half a world away. I have no doubt the accompanying letter casually said she happened to drop across the papers whilst cleaning her drawer out. Father would add his laconic, yet heartfelt greeting as a post script.

But all went well and the telegram duly arrived that a daughter had been born. That very evening I saw mother wiping her pen nib to make the eighth entry in the family Bible. This family Bible was a wedding present from her old teacher and friend, Miss Yeend and most of the entries in the frontispiece are in mother's clear and meticulous hand and she had proudly recorded the first entry, "Our Wedding Day August 18th 1904". All our births were, in turn, faithfully entered and, of course, the entries now reach far down the page. Against the entry for the birth of my brother John on April 26th 1908 my father had written "snow on the ground 6 inches deep." April 26'th was usually about the date of the Cup Final and, to us, snow on that date ought to have been out of the question. Nevertheless my father's side note was there in black and white. I am afraid the family had many jokes and questions of this feature of John's birthday.

However, as recently as 1985 Margaret and I were visiting a stately home in Staffordshire at Hoar Cross, the home of the Meynell family. In the study we found that the owner had religiously kept detailed weather records since the turn of the century. Temperature, barometer pressures, rainfall — everything. There were stacks of the large leather bound volumes and, of course, we selected the appropriate one, turned the pages back to April 26th 1908 and there we found the entry "8″ snow overnight". How pleased we were and how pleased father would have been to say "I told you so". We might have been tempted to counter and suggest he was 2″ out in his assessment of depth.

* * * *

Mother was always a keen and efficient knitter. Although quite able to do so, she did not go in for the larger garments such as jumpers and sweaters, but concentrated, more or less, in keeping up her menfolk's stock of socks. They were always knitted, I understand, knit one purl one and as we watched the length of the sock grow it amused us to know when she was "just going to turn the heel". She knitted on four steel needles and the speed with which she proceeded was very surprising, the needles making that regular and peculiar clicking noise. She was able to knit even in the dark or without the need to glance down. In the early days of the cinema, when she had to take Ena and John, she used not to be interested in the film and so took her knitting with her and probably completed a whole sock during the performance. The socks produced were about half length and, if truth were really known, they were not all that comfortable, because there was, until later, no turnover provided to house a garter. Consequently the socks tended to concertina down to the ankles. I can hear my brother now, unseen, running along the street, and occasionally his footsteps would momentarily stop, and I knew then that he would be pulling up his socks. Another feature of mother's knitted socks was that they were knitted in a fairly wide range of blues, greens and greys except, of course, our white cricket and ringed rugger ones. In those days, before indistructable socks, holes seemed to appear quite frequently at the heel and it was unthinkable that we went about showing them. Mother darned them quite often, but then found it was more sensible to cut the whole foot off entirely, pick up the stitches, and refoot them. The only drawback to this method was that we walked about in socks the foot and half the ankle of which differed widely in colour. Cricket socks had to be treated likewise because the heat generated in our boots from days in the field and with frequent washing turned the wool into something of a dense mass which we called "bulls ears'. But in these cases we did insist that only white wool was used.

We did not steer clear of all the labours involved in the production of socks because we were hauled in to help with the winding of the wool and I have suffered aching arms in so doing. One had to achieve a successful rhythm with the tilting of the hands and release of the thumb to keep the person winding fully occupied without check. Eventually a series of spinning wooden wool winders were tried out which were very efficient and quickened the matter up considerably and at the same time released the second person to get on with something else. Then old abandoned garments were sometimes unravelled for the wool to be recycled. In this case duties were reversed for we, then, were the winders with the ever growing ball of crinkly wool in our hands whilst mother controlled and sometimes juggled with the stitches as they came apart.

* * * *

Although mother could not enthuse over films, which she dismissed as being "far fetched" she was a keen theatre goer and loved a good play. I have

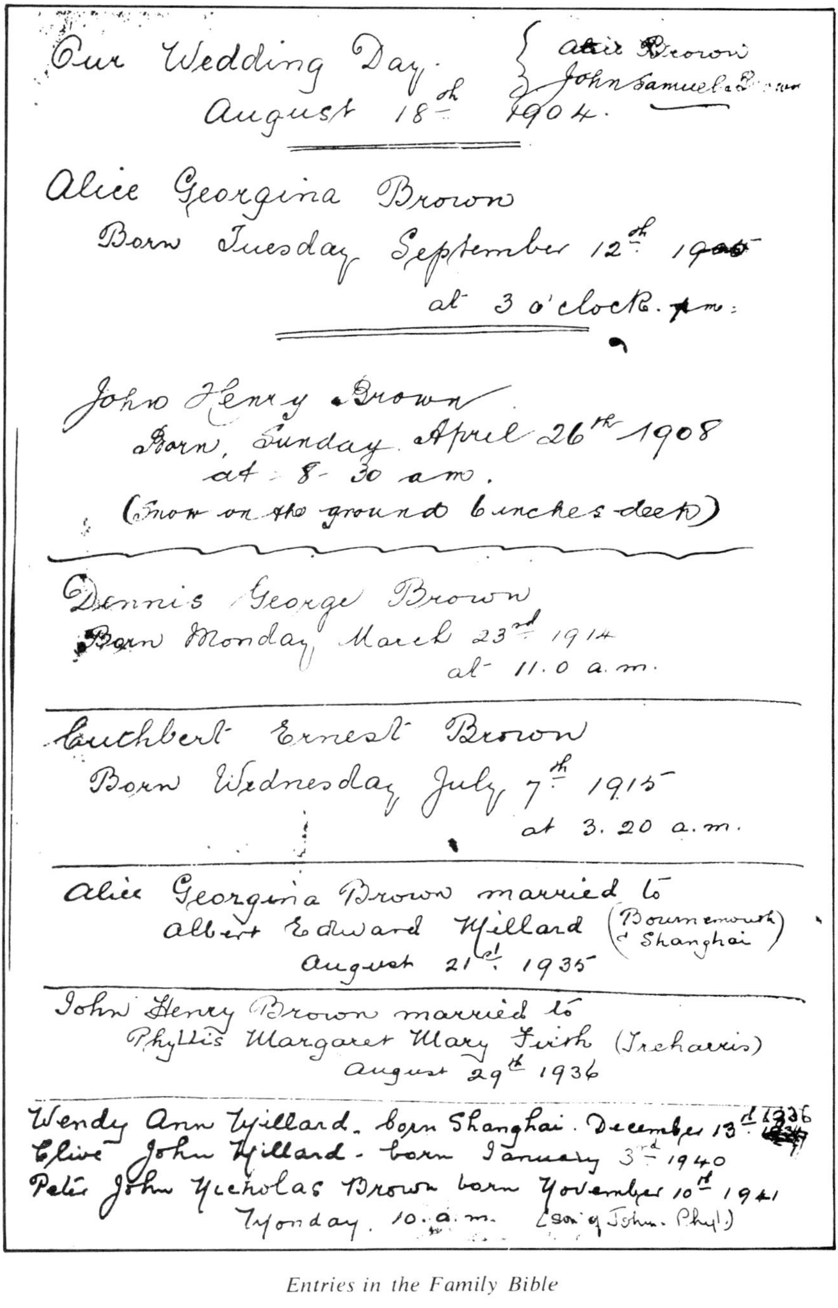

Our Wedding Day { Alice Brown / John Samuel Brown }
August 18th 1904.

Alice Georgina Brown
Born Tuesday September 12th 1905
at 3 o'clock. am.

John Henry Brown
Born, Sunday April 26th 1908
at 8-30 a.m.
(Snow on the ground 6 inches deep)

Dennis George Brown
Born Monday March 23rd 1914
at 11.0 a.m.

Cuthbert Ernest Brown
Born Wednesday July 7th 1915
at 3.20 a.m.

Alice Georgina Brown married to
Albert Edward Willard (Bournemouth & Shanghai)
August 21st 1935

John Henry Brown married to
Phyllis Margaret Mary Frith (Treharris)
August 29th 1936

Wendy Ann Willard. born Shanghai. December 13th 1936
Clive John Willard - born January 3rd 1940
Peter John Nicholas Brown born November 10th 1941
Monday. 10. a.m. (son of John. Phyl.)

Entries in the Family Bible

The circus comes to town in Bore Street

little doubt that she and father attended many in London before their family came along and, of course, afterwards whenever the opportunity arose. She saw the early productions of the Sherlock Holmes Plays, possibly when Charlie Chaplin was in the cast, and she would tell us about the intense drama achieved on the stage in, such as, 'The Speckled Band'.

But generally the citizens in Lichfield were restricted to performances by the travelling theatre who set up their portable premises on the same field which received all the circus's. This theatre was owned and run by one Mr. Whacker Holloway and it was the event of the season, playing to packed houses. Their 'piece de resistance' was, of course, "Maria Marten and the murder in the Red Barn". Father always told the story of one of the actors who considered himself to be rather superior and boasted that when he entered the stage his superior ability and flair would be immediately apparent. One of the lesser mortals duly made his entry and said his piece "the Count is wow-n-did mi lord" to which our superior friend answered "not see-rye-usly I 'ope".

In her early days mother never missed a circus and used to attend with her brothers. I suppose the keeping of horses for the bread rounds stimulated the wish to be with all the animals. Accordingly, whenever we visited the local circus we would return home full of the surprising skills of the artistes and the animals. She listened with interest but usually said "they do nothing new."

* * * *

Later in these memoirs I shall mention the life of sport in which I took part and which mother, although staying at home could not avoid becoming involved. She was not a sports lady, as such, but she gave us every encouragement to partake, except in one respect That exception was boxing. This sport horrified her and we would have to keep it from her when we were involved in the House Competitions at School. To her disgust she once heard one of the boxing commentators on the radio, probably Barrington Dalby, say "Oh what a beautiful punch". Many times after that she referred to this allegedly outrageous statement. In her eyes no punch could be beautiful.

But she had given father her full support and interest in the sports he had undertaken and did so fully with us. Whenever we set out to play in a rugger match she would, without fail and with a twinkle in her eye, say "If they want the ball let them have it". Of course she knew nothing could have been further from our intentions. Yet when we returned home she would always inquire as to whether we had won or, in summer, ask how many runs we had made. In addition to this there was always that quick glance to see if we had sustained any injury. Usually if we had received some knock or other or pulled a muscle we would keep it to ourselves and her only way of finding out was, secretly, to watch us as we climbed the stairs. She claimed, probably correctly, that this was the time any difficulty of movement would show itself. But it didn't show the purple circular bruises on our thighs sustained whilst batting and which we kept concealed until we took the liniment into the bathroom when we were getting ready for bed. But we didn't get away with it for mother, coming up later, would enquire the reason for the smell of embrocation. Our secret would then be out and she would demand to see the bruises and be horrified at their colour and extent. No doubt she would report to father all about it who would probably question how it was, with a bat in our hands, we had let the ball hit us!

Curiously, the only sport in which she really held an interest was the Boat Race. We could never understand why she so strongly supported Cambridge and always willed them to win. Whenever they did so she always provided the family with a pound of Mackintosh's Toffees. We did well out of this for of the seventeen races rowed from 1920 Cambridge won sixteen and, accordingly, this toffee reward became an assured annual event.

* * * *

Mother tended to be very local in her ways and interests, yet relished visits to London where she would take full advantage of a day's shopping at Selfridges, Gamages and the other large stores. She took great pride in the Royal Family and, if we were in London with her, it was essential to stand and admire Buckingham Palace. When the National Anthem was played we were made to stand firmly at attention wherever we happened to be. It seems hard to believe, for even if the bars struck up on the radio in our own drawing room, up we would all stand. But times and attitudes change, for then, when proceding in a bus along Whitehall we passed The Cenotaph with hats raised and heads bowed and, of course, on November 11th we would freeze at 11.00 a.m. and I would hear the distant rat-tat-a-tat of The Royal Scot heading north just a few miles away to the east and wonder why someone hadn't brought it to a standstill. It was also quite essential that we attended the Remembrance Sunday Service at the Cathedral.

It was probably mother's pride in Country and Empire that took us all up to London for the British Empire Exhibition in 1924 at Wembley. We went only for the day and I remember the Wembley turf accommodating five, I think it was, circus rings, all operating at the same time and we found it difficult to concentrate on any particular ring or performer.

She kept abreast of the country's events and was proud of national achievements much, I suppose, as we admire Concorde or the Queen Elizabeth II. Thus it was with the Titanic and she would tell, often, what a wonderful ship it was and how they had been assured it was unsinkable. When the news of the disaster came through it must have been such a great shock to her, both as regards the ship and the number of souls lost. But I could understand how she felt for we, as boys, later on, felt the same such horror when the R.101 crashed on a hill in France.

It may be that the influence of the Titanic roused, in some way, mother's interest in the National Lifeboat Association because it was this charity upon which she gave much time and helped to organise all the whist drives and other fund raising events for this particular cause. It always struck us as unusual that this institution attracted her appeal having in mind that Lichfield was as far from the coast, in any direction, as could be.

* * * *

Mother led an active life, busy with her family, supporting her husband in his activities. At this time household aids were not numerous and menial tasks had to be completed daily. Even in her then modern home there were many open grates and a kitchen range, all of which needed to be cleared, re-laid and re-kindled.

Cooking was carried out on a coal fired range which had to be kept going all day, even in summer, because it provided the hot water. The red quarries on the kitchen floor, although laid smooth and well were not conducive to easy cleaning. But I am pleased that mother was always able to afford a help which obviously relieved her of some heavy slogging. Mother had to be careful of the arrangements in this respect because I remember that father generally complained that the help engaged was always in his way!

Afternoons would then be free for mother to take it rather more easily after lunch when she could sit and carry on with her mending or her knitting, visit friends and attend the functions to which she was related in the town. Her time was always well occupied and she was horrified to hear someone say to her that taking the dog a walk "put an hour or so in". Like her husband and family she would have wished for an hour or two more in most days. Quite often, though, she would have need to retire to her bedroom and rest. She was a great believer in smelling salts, which were always available at her bedside, to relieve her headaches.

Mother lived to a ripe old age and in her last days, when she was confined to her bed, she lay content, yet conscious that her bedroom and all about her had to be clean and immaculate in the way she had always insisted, and her concern was that she was not being a nuisance. Years earlier she had nursed her dying sister and even on that last day had been taking tea together, much as they would have done earlier in their lives with their own mother in the sitting room behind the bakers shop. Clean freshly ironed table napkins were on the tray and her sister had said "proud to the last Alice" and so it was with mother. I was not there but her last words, I know, would have been "thank you" — a gentle woman to the last who had radiated tenderness and goodness throughout her life.

Chapter Six

HOLIDAY INTERLUDE

FROM an early age I was fortunate, each year, to be taken for a summer holiday away from home, usually to the seaside. The family were never taken to the southern resorts but to the Lancashire and North Wales coasts due to their comparative nearness and the convenient main line railway service. The very early holidays were spent at Blackpool and we were joined there for many years by cousins, the Hammersleys, a family of three.

We were thrilled when the taxi, or cab as father called it, rolled up at the door to take us down to Trent Valley Station. I remember well the excitement as we clambered aboard and found little tip-up seats, just behind the driver, all to ourselves, and how the doors and the windows in their wooden frames rattled as we trundled through the heavy grinding gears and sped through the town.

On the train, as we neared Blackpool, we would peer ahead through the carriage window and see, on the skyline, the familiar and outstanding landmark of the tower and, just near it, the big wheel. Once there we lost no time in getting down to the beach and, with seven children, all was activity and towers and castles quickly rose from the sand and, later, as we developed our skills, really huge animals were heaped up and sculptured. We were all so proud of one large elephant lying there as if at the end of a safari and we stood smartly to attention as we were photographed. Our clothing on the beach was remarkable and though a hot afternoon we would remain fully dressed with no thought of baring our backs. A far cry from the scantilly dressed holidaymakers of today.

Some of our later holidays at Blackpool were about the time Gracie Fields was starting her career and attended her performances at the Palace. Afterwards we waited to see her as she emerged on to the front where she was cheered with much enthusiasm. I remember her hair being so dark, parted in the middle with headphone plaited buns over each ear.

But gradually our holidays concentrated on Rhyl where we stayed each year at the same self-catering apartments in a street leading from the front, one Sandringham Avenue. Rhyl, in those early post First World War years was very much more quiet and secluded but, as have many other resorts, moved with the times and altered its facilities to attract visitors.

Pierrots, today, appear to have disappeared yet, a purpose built outdoor theatre housed the Jolly Boys and there would be very few vacant deck chairs for their performances. Band concerts, too, in the marine gardens where we sat and listened to Gilbert and Sullivan melodies as the Sunday evening tide went out just beyond. And, when we were at the period early bedtime was not essential we would troop along the east promenade to enjoy Billy Manders with his Quaintesques.

On other days father would have arranged for us to go on a charabanc trip in the North Wales hinterland. The vehicle was very basic. High and open we were exposed to the elements but it did have a moveable canvas framed hood which could be hauled over us if we had been caught in a skud of rain. The seats stretched fully across the width of the vehicle with a door, on the footpath side, to each row. The seats themselves were soft and comfortable and covered with real leather.

I see us all seated ready for going, my sister, with shingled hair and conspicuous flapper style white head band, John in white cotton shirt, hair well greased and combed well back while we two small brothers have on our usual buttoned up jerseys and, even on holiday, our small navy blue caps. Mother holds her head low in a knitted close fitting and wind resisting hat and to complete our family picture father sits, confidently on the back of a seat, ready for a buffeting in the wind, in a raincoat and smartly styled trilby hat with a ribboned edging round an upturned brim. In all there are about thirty passengers, only a few without head dresses, looking forward to their drive into the sunshine of Wales some sixty-five years ago.

Brooke Brothers have modestly painted their name on the white body with the driver waiting to drive off in this cumbersome vehicle. His was no easy task to manoeuvre around the severe corners leading to Swallow Falls and Bettys Coed and, perhaps, even as far as the Great Orme or the Horse Shoe Pass in other directions. The ride was always a bumpy one for the tyres were solid and inflexible. Communication tended to be by signs as the noise of the engine vied with the buffeting of the wind and, in the main, we sat each with our own thoughts until some particular landmark was reached with much gesticulation. Back at Rhyl we would clamber down and the little family group would make their way to the "digs" with mother just remembering to call at the little bread shop on the corner to buy a large custard pie to eat with our meal later on.

Such were our holidays at the seaside which we always enjoyed despite the strange atmosphere of unfamiliar rooms where the sun shone across from unexpected directions. We found it strange, too, to be arranging whole days to involve all the family rather than the day just happening as it did at home where everyone generally went their own ways, knowing that we would all gather together again at meal times.

* * * *

Father had many business contacts in and around the Lichfield locality and had need for consultations over income tax advice and insurance matters. Many were personal friends and, as a family, we made frequent visits with him. Sometimes during an evening, perhaps for Sunday afternoon tea and occasionally we stayed for a few days or even a week. These visits were to become quite a feature of our holidays. One farm, in particular, became a regular summer occasion. It was the Manor Farm at Harlaston, some 10 miles from Lichfield. Our means of locomotion was a 1914 B.S.A. belt driven motor cycle combination. The bike was fairly reliable except that in wet weather the belt slipped badly and progress was retarded. After a final check of the magneto spark and the oil levels father would draw up at the gate. We would be rounded up, not without suppressed excitement at the thought of a week on a farm. We would then take up our various positions: Ena and John sat astride the pillion seat behind father. There were plenty of brackets and bars to obtain a foothold but the main security was found in clasping arms around each other. When my father gained some momentum on the straighter roads all three would lean forward into the wind with my sister gripping the curious plaited leather belt which father wore over his motoring jacket. Mother and Dennis would sit side by side on the official seat of the open sidecar, mother on the side nearest to the bike in order that she could translate and transmit father's instructions to the pillion riders. This suited my brother who then had a less interrupted view to the front and to the side. For myself I sat in front of them in the nose of the sidecar on a square Peak Freans biscuit tin. There was a small door which allowed us all to get in and out. Mother would have to be seated before I could get in with my biscuit tin and then all safely installed father would slam the little door before going round to mount the motorbike.

The nose in which I sat was shaped rather like that of an advanced passenger train and my legs intermingled with all the odd items we were taking with us. Looking back now over the years I have come to realise my position was the most vulnerable for had we happened to run into anything I would have been the first "to go for a Burton". Even so John had to make sure he didn't fall off at the back of the pillion. With a clatter and several misfire bangs father would start the engine going and with a last glance all round we would set off down the street in the direction of the town.

But, reaching Lichfield, we had to stop at the post office which, at that time, was situated in Bird Street just past Minster Pool. Father always had much mail to despatch. This halt would give us time to make necessary adjustments to our travelling positions and exchange a few words prior to the dusty and noisy journey, hopefully non-stop, in front of us. Eventually father would appear, slip the letters in the posting box, climb back on to the motor cycle and off we would start again. Once outside the town on the Tamworth and Whittington Road the bike soon got into its stride and the beat of the exhaust rose up at the side of the sidecar. We all sat back busy with our own thoughts as the wind rushed against our faces.

Meanwhile, we had chugged past Whittington Heath and Whittington itself on through to Hademore. Here we all sat up with some anticipation because the main L.M.S. line from Euston crossed our road with a level crossing. My father would, no doubt, have preferred the gates to be open so that he could press on to Harleston without having to stop, but we were quite satisfied if the large white gates were across the road blocking our path.

Main line trains were frequent and it gave us quite a thrill to be halted close up to the gates feeling quite secure as the locomotives loomed up and thundered by with the carriages screaming and rat-tat-tatting behind. But there was another aspect of the track at this point which gave us an added thrill. The land, and, therefore, the track, was very level hereabouts and, for this reason, water picking up troughs were installed in the centre of the lines. With a great roar and a sustained hiss the engines would take up water and huge plumes of spray would be thrown out, making the ballast quite wet and reaching down to the crossing. Quite often we also had to wait while a heavy goods moved on in the opposite direction and we counted the number of trucks as it pondered by. Eventually the sound of the trains would subside into the distance. The signal box was situated by the side of the track and the crossing gates were controlled therefrom. We could hear the bells ring in the box and watch as the

Early Blackpool

Blackpool Sands

With mother and a friend

On safari

Band Stand in Marine Gardens, Rhyl

Rhyl sands and Pavilion

Charabanc trip

signalman swung over his levers. This was the signal also for father to start up the bike again. At Elmhurst further up the line the signalman, at this stage, had to leave his box to clatter down the steps to open the gates himself but here at Hademore the signalman was able to control the gates whilst still in his box by winding a large handwheel mechanism. Father lost no time in getting across the line and mother would look apprehensively up and down the track. With a wave to the signalman we would be on our way again.

We would look out for two other features we always enjoyed. The first was the mile wall. It flanked one of the Earl of Lichfield's estates and as we sat in the sidecar only feet away from this brick wall it seemed endless and the more so because there were bends and turns in its length. At last we saw the White Lodge ahead which signalled the end of it and almost immediately afterwards we came to a series of small hump-backed bridges leading to two major arched spans adjacent to each other over the River Tame. As passengers we could admire the pleasant structure of the bridges and the parapets but father had need to keep his eye on the road because the junction beyond was not without hazards even with the very little traffic about. Quite soon, after negotiating the corner, he would point ahead and indicate we were nearly there. The cluster of buildings just coming into view was Harlaston and we were soon driving along its only street bending round past the Church before turning sharply into the yard of the Manor Farm in some triumph.

Having heard our approach our farmer friend approached, with a broad smile. "Have you come to see 'wi faircies'?" (our faces) he would say. We were a little slow in leaving our cramped positions as we had hardly moved for an hour, but we soon had the farm dogs muzzling around us as we made our way to the rear entrance of the farmhouse.

Once there we had the freedom of the place, apart from one or two clear restrictions, which our parents ensured we observed. I remember Mrs. Lees, the farmer's wife, produced a small bucket of milk and a ladle, "for the children, on condition they don't chase the cats". We enjoyed ourselves as only one can around a farm amongst all the ricks and the barns and the animals. The occupations of the grown-ups was far more sedate and father would produce his camera and we would be lined up in the little front flower garden specially attired in our sailor suits for the occasion or we would go down to the orchard to pose. After much explanation Mr. Lees would be entrusted to take the snap. I see my father and mother in that orchard of yester-year not more than forty years old, happy with their family around them. Father had forsaken his shooting jacket and breeches, his hair still dark though receding, and mother in her smart white blouse and dark skirt. Ena, growing up now, in tweed skirt with John not yet growing out of the familiar style of jersey we were all to wear. His hand bandaged, injured probably, in some prank he had been up to that morning. The photograph taken is before me as I write and I feel my father's supporting arm about me as if it were only yesterday. Mr. Lees would leave us for awhile and suddenly appear astride one of his horses, a black mare. This gave a further opportunity for father and we were all taken mounted on the horse both in the orchard and later in the yard. For myself I was not too fond of the animal yet I was inveigled into holding the reins for a photograph with Ena in the saddle but I kept the horse well at arms length. I did not feel too secure either when the three brothers were taken together, as the ground to me seemed to be such a long way down.

Mr. Lees himself was an odd bird. A reasonably successful tenant farmer he had many idiosyncracies and father would tell us later that he could not suffer fools gladly and some of his stronger opinions tended to embarrass. Yet despite this he was full of fun and smiles and shared many a joke with father. It amused him to wake us up early by throwing small apples against our bedroom window. I suppose he had been up hours and thought it was time we stirred. He was lame in one leg yet managed to get about his farm and rode to hounds regularly. He rode in a bowler hat and a smart dark Norfolk jacket and breeches yet, when attending to his farm duties, he wore an old brown dust jacket tied at the waist with string and, in summer, an old straw brimmer. His wife was very placid and gave the impression of submitting to his every whim and enduring a hard life.

It was during one such holiday that we were introduced to the novelty of the motor car. Friends of the Lees called with their two seater Humber. All the family lined up to be taken for rides up and down the village street. Compared with the car of today it was cumbersome with a heavy wooden steering wheel, large, but ornate, lamps and an artillery type spare wheel mounted on the off running board which enforced the driver to gain access from the passenger side. Although there was a boot of sorts the portable hood hung well over it and there was, thus, no space for a dicky seat.

But I remember most the evening tours of the farm in the float. Mother usually stayed behind with Mrs. Lees and got on with her knitting and they may well have strolled in the front garden or down to the orchard before Mrs. Lees fed the cats and tied the dogs up in the stable for the night. We all clambered into the float to sit on the wooden planks thrown across from side to side. After the comparative smoothness of the tyres of the motorbike the wheels of the float were harsh and made a grinding noise along the road. We were keen to get on but I remember the float pulling up alongside an old barn in obvious need of repair and, in between grumbles about his landlord, old Lees expostulated at some length to father how a builder had let him down. Father confided to us, afterwards, that he was glad he was not in the builder's shoes. But soon we had turned off the road and headed across the farm from the gate of one field to the next, irrespective, it appeared, as to whether we were over pasture or crops. Occasionally we saw a rabbit and Mr. Lees remarked that they ought to have brought a gun with them. I am sure we children and father were pleased the gun had been left behind for safety reasons, having in mind there were six of us filling the float. I have mentioned that Mr. Lees was lame and because of this on any shooting expedition he always remained in the float and shot from it. We had good cause, therefore, to be thankful, but it did occur to us in later years, and father agreed, that the horse pulling the float was likely to take a peppering as Mr. Lees followed a low flying pheasant in his sights and we could imagine the animal's ears would be pretty well punctured.

By this time it had become quite chilly and the four of us huddled together on our seats and were glad to realise that he had turned for home for the low sun was now setting and glowing behind us. By the time we reached the village street it was getting quite dark and difficult to distinguish the usual landmarks, although the small tower of the Church loomed up and we knew we were not

The old B.S.A. with John, Dennis and Ena

The old Post Office in Bird Street

At Manor Farm, Harlaston

Ena and myself — at arms length!

All aboard

Farmer Lees

The old Humber

far from the farm. We turned in at the yard to see the lights of the outhouses where mother was silhouetted against them. She had heard the horse clip clopping down the road and was anxious to see that we were all back safely. We were ushered into the kitchen where the inevitable milk was on the table for us near a pile of sandwiches.

On other evenings we stayed indoors and we would listen to the conversation in the little sitting room. But more often than not old Lees, with a satisfied smile, would lean down behind the piano and pull out two violin cases. My father was easily persuaded to take one of the violins and join him. Ena struggled to accompany them on the upright piano. Struggled because the keys were stiff and the piano was not kept in tune and because the performers on the violins were hesitant and unsure; although, when the resin had been found and after several attempts, they scraped through the Elfin Waltz with a pleasant swing.

My brother and I would then be bustled off to bed and we would giggle upstairs about the abortive initial attempts at the music and as we lay there we could hear muffled conversation and laughter from below. We were old enough to know that, after our dismissal, Mr. Lees would go to the cupboard on the wall and offer father something a little stronger to drink.

Also staying at the farm was a relative of the Lees, an elderly man whose hand shook so badly that he drank his tea through a tube, much to our young surprise and intent examination. At night he would climb the stairs with a candle in his hand and we would lie awake waiting for his light to appear, because it threw an unsteady dancing shadow of the banisters across the little glass fanlight over the doorway of our bedroom and we knew it was him.

It may be, towards the end of the week, we started to wonder what was going on at home and we would not be too unhappy when we all clambered aboard the old bike and set off back. We would take our usual interest in the familiar landmarks and sometimes we would travel on a different route through Elford, but we were all pleased when we sailed down Saint John Street and the old exhaust barked and resounded under the railway bridge. We usually had a competition to see who would be the first to recognise someone we knew in the Street and we had guesses as to whom that person might be. Year after year it turned out to be much the same few persons in their daily haunts and one fellow was usually favourite, perhaps because his grey beard was so prominent as his head lolled to one side. This Mr. Hughes sang in the choir at St. Chad's.

And then back at home we would lose no time in running into the garden and be surprised to find it all so unfamiliar after our absence and see how the grass had grown and where, a week ago, when we had been called together, we had thrown down the old tennis racquet with which we had been playing. The rooms, too, seemed strange because the ceilings at the farm had been so much lower. But we all soon settled into normal routines; father had to catch up with his post and, whilst mother checked through her needs in the pantry, Ena reassured herself by rattling through her favourite piece on our more familiar piano. Later, as mother said goodnight to us, she expressed the opinion "There was nothing like being back in your own bed".

Chapter Seven

THE GREENHILL BOWER

ANYONE who has lived in Lichfield, even for the shortest length of time, will be aware of the affection with which the Greenhill Bower is held. It is called the Greenhill Bower because of its original location on this open space, which, used to be quite an extensive paved area, with a large horse drinking trough in the centre, all at the junction of Tamworth Street, George Lane, Rotten Row and Church Street. Our young minds had difficulty in dissociating this Greenhill with the one in the hymn, "There is a greenhill far away, without a city wall". We could not understand why greenhill was sung to be so far away and why it had not got a city wall! But all was clarified in due course.

But the origins of the Bower started here on our Greenhill. The Bower House has been erected here each Whit Monday for centuries and the ceremony of the garlands and bowers enacted thereabouts.

The Bower of today is held, to suit other considerations, on the Spring Bank Holiday. Almost without fail those Whit Monday Bowers were scorching hot, sun filled days. For the whole of that weekend, including the Tuesday, the Market Square and Greenhill were almost entirely closed to traffic and for Bower Day itself further sideshows came in and spread into the whole of the town centre. Train loads of people arrived at the City Station from all over the Midlands and the Black Country and from an early hour the streets would be choc-a-bloc. All the public houses were given licence to keep open for the whole day. The procession in the middle of the day is still the highlight and makes a circuitous journey through the city streets including even the precincts of the Cathedral and the Close and people stand to watch some five or six deep. In the afternoon the athletic sports were held in the recreation grounds.

The history of the Bower dates back centuries to Courts of Arraye when, instead of maintaining a standing army, men capable of carrying arms were mustered and counted each Whit Monday. Special constables or dozeners were appointed to report the number available. After a parade through the streets the men gathered at Greenhill for refreshments and, no doubt, this led to the erection of the Bower House and the present day distribution of Bower cakes. With the end of the Civil War a standing army was established and there was no longer any need for the Court of Arraye. But, combining other ancient flower festivals and exhibitions of local crafts, festivities have continued on this day in the form of the Bower we know today.

* * * *

My father took an active part in the organisation and preparation of the Bower for a period of over sixty years. In this way it was quickly brought home to us the immense amount of voluntary work necessary for an event of this size. From the previous autumn Bower Committee enthusiasts and volunteers are organised and channelled into the many and various sub-committees and the whole broad aspect of the Bower arranged to the last detail. As the great day neared pressures increased. The Committee had a longstanding tenancy of a yard in Frog Lane. This yard had been owned by a Mr. Levett and was originally called Levetts Yard. Similarly he owned the large fields flanking Station Road which, in turn, were called Levetts Fields, a name still held today. This Bower Yard was, indeed, the engine room of the whole concept. It was here that all the properties, models, scenery, bunting, flags, paint, timber and all the thousand and one necessary items were kept. The portable Bower House itself was also stored here and only released for its annual outing to Greenhill. The tableaux were built mainly in this yard and from dawn in the days prior to Whitsun it would be alive with activity. Father would only just manage to get back home for a hurried breakfast before attending to his own business. All the vehicles used for tableaux in the procession were, at this time, horse drawn and much negotiation, to ensure they were available, was undertaken with local business concerns, chief of which, was the City Brewery Company who had a string of horses and drays for their deliveries. Horses had an advantage in a procession because they could walk very slowly or be halted without difficulty. On the other hand they too had to be decorated and this only a few hours before setting off.

The setting up of the fairgrounds themselves was an essential work of art for, with such huge machines and associated equipment it was not a simple task to calculate the space required, having in mind the confined and irregular areas available. Showmen would not take kindly to being told, on arrival, there was no room for them.

At home we were fully aware of all these difficulties for we would hear father mentioning them at most mealtimes during this hectic period. We, ourselves, did our best to assist and make ourselves available as and when required.

* * * *

The Bower proper started for us on the Whit Sunday morning when we all attended St. Michael's Church for the official Bower Service. The Mayor and Corporation walked the half mile or so in procession led, inevitably, by the City Band. Military contingents from Whittington Barracks were also drafted into the parade. The Rector, the Reverend Percy Howard, who was Bower Chaplain, from the pulpit welcomed all these distinguished guests and preached a usual sermon on the values of tradition in the community.

In the evening we would again set off into the town to the Market Square which, already almost full with roundabouts, swings and all the other equipment, provided just enough space to hold an outdoor Bower Service. It was a unique service conducted with appropriate reverence by the Bower chaplain from the front platform of the merry-go-round motor cars. It was so strange to hear the huge fairground organ mechanically trundling through the hymns we had only heard before in the confines of church; yet here we were striking up with loud outdoor voices with the organ adding many cymbal noises and tinklings which were not attainable, or even allowed, in church. A reading and a few prayers interposed and gradually the service was blended into a welcome to the Bower. Mr. Pat Collins, head of the fairground organisation, was welcomed and he, in turn, wished success to the Bower for the sake of the charities which would benefit, the enjoyment of the populace and, no doubt, for the sake of his members whose livelihood it was to operate the machines and sideshows. During the final hymn the setting sun would bless the scene from across the square as its rays caught the top of St. Mary's spire above us and then everyone would turn away for home and pick their way through the Sunday silent sideshows quite pleased with the message of the service and anticipating the great day tomorrow.

* * * *

In our household Bower Day itself started early as father would be down at the yard by dawn checking final arrangements. The day's events were on a tight schedule and helpers would have little time to spare and few would be able to attend the Court of Arraye in the middle of the morning. Activity was intense on Levetts Fields and Station Road where the first tableaux were already arriving to be marshalled into position ready to start in the procession.

At the head of the procession a banner was carried proclaiming in large letters "Welcome to the Bower". It was carried by two outwalkers held aloft on poles and even in the slightest breeze they struggled along and had need to lean forward to make proper progress and, at the same time, keep the banner at a level, readable keel. Following this banner was, according to the official programme, "a Citizen on Horseback". The citizen has always to be well-known and turned out immaculately dressed. In the twenties this citizen was Mr. Tommy Charrington. The main qualification for the position, apart from being able to ride the horse, was the ability to puff large cigars for the duration of the procession. Following him would be the Lichfield City Band. This, together with the shouting and clapping of the spectators, caused the horse to go along jigging and fretting sideways for most of the way and the citizen may have had some reservations as to whether he had been wise in taking the job on.

But the main part of the procession consisted of about five tableaux — this word was used in preference to the more modern term 'floats' and seems to have been handed down from the more ancient parades of posies and bowers. They were the outcome of months of dedicated design and construction, yet on the day, in a few minutes they passed by and the crowds turned to look for the next one. Themes were selected each year perhaps, 'Nursery Rhymes', 'The Seasons of the Year', 'Old Street Cries', 'International Scenes — Old English, Dutch, Japanese or Venetian'. All subjects which lent themselves to the imagination, ingenuity and decorative skills of the members of the Committee. Interposed were smaller entries, decorated bicycles and heavy comic figures mounted on the shoulders of unlucky and perspiring volunteers. The figures were rather grotesque and caricatured policemen, farmers, heavy weight boxers and even Harold Lloyd. To keep the whole thing on the move various bands blared through all the well known military marches. They were led by the ever present City Band with military bands from the local barracks and those from neighbouring districts. Chasetown Colliery Silver Band often came down but care had to be taken to ensure they were well behind the City Band as there was some rivalry and there had been some suggestion of the poaching of players.

* * * *

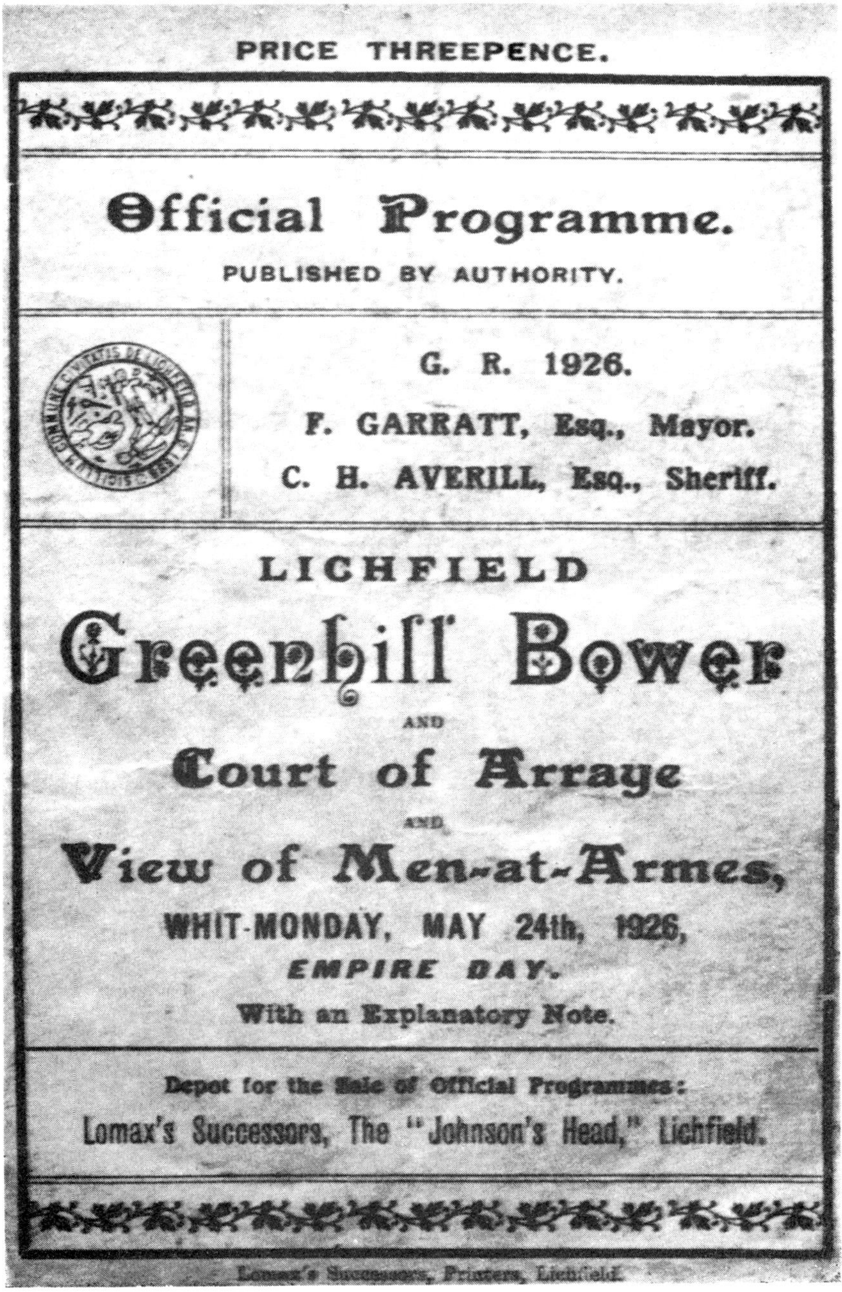

PRICE THREEPENCE.

Official Programme.

PUBLISHED BY AUTHORITY.

G. R. 1926.

F. GARRATT, Esq., Mayor.

C. H. AVERILL, Esq., Sheriff.

LICHFIELD

Greenhill Bower

AND

Court of Arraye

AND

View of Men-at-Armes,

WHIT-MONDAY, MAY 24th, 1926,

EMPIRE DAY.

With an Explanatory Note.

Depot for the Sale of Official Programmes:

Lomax's Successors, The "Johnson's Head," Lichfield.

Lomax's Successors, Printers, Lichfield.

Bower Programme. Empire Day 1926

Early Bower Tableau inspired by The Wright Brothers

Dr. Johson bi-centenary tableau 1909

It was inevitable that father would rope in my brothers and myself for an entry in the procession. In 1924 he had a brainwave to decorate his old B.S.A. motorbike combination as a steeplechase with the three of us as jockeys and the winning horse being named Bower 1924. The sidecar itself was removed entirely leaving only the frame of the chassis and the wheel. On this was fixed two borrowed rocking horses taken off their stands. I was to be mounted on the sidecar horse with Dennis on the one just behind leaping a fence whilst John, who was to drive the bike, was riding the winner in the form of a horse styled around the bike itself, with the head stretching just past the winning post mounted up from the front wheel. A photograph exists and on close examination many faults could be suggested but, at the time, it was accepted as a good effort provided the varying sizes of the horses heads and other details were ignored. We were not too pleased in having to wear ladies bloomers adapted for our breeches which kept coming loose at our knees despite large safety pins and we also thought the brown paper leggings might have been constructed of something more realistic. We may also have felt a bit foolish, but on the other hand we were quite chuffed when a neighbour or relation in the crowd recognised us and shouted words of encouragement. During the journey round one technical difficulty arose for which provision had not been considered and that was the speed with which we moved. Obviously to accommodate various pedestrian entries and horses and in order that spectators might have sufficient time to study us as we went by, the pace was essentially a slow one. The motorbike was more used to being driven along at a rattling good pace and, being air cooled, by the time we were halfway round the engine was showing signs of overheating. Father had instructed John, before we started, to keep to the regular pace of the others and to keep well back from the entry in front which allowed us no leeway. But with various strategic cut outs and free wheeling John kept the thing going with some skill and much credit.

* * * *

When we were not directly involved we watched the procession with mother, from a position at the Close Corner, for hereabouts the ground was higher. We were able to look along and over the heads of the crowds the whole length of Bird Street. As we looked the 'Welcome to the Bower' banner had just appeared by the Swan Hotel swaying high with its bold lettering, braid and tassles. The thumping beat of the City Band broke through and as it approached we recognised the old familiar Bower march "will you, won't you, will you, won't you come to the Bower". All the children in the town and many grown-ups made a point of chanting it for weeks before, and after, the great event. The Band played it unashamedly in that peculiar way whereby the trombones loudly proclaimed the oomp pah and left the rest of the Band to come in with the "will you, won't you" part. But just past the Garden of Remembrance the big drummer double beated them to stop and have a breather. Yet this did not prevent the crowds surging forward to obtain better views or for a ripple of clapping to break out along the lines as the head of the procession reached them. The banner, carried along strangely quiet without the band, swung into the Cathedral Close where there were less spectators. Here Tommy Charrington recognised mother and for once gathering his horse together into a sedate walk, doffed his top hat high above his head and swung it down to the horses flanks in an exaggerated show of recognition. Slightly embarrassed, mother allowed him a reticent smile and a slight bow of the head. But the City Band, now also reaching the corner and having made full use of their breather, then gave full vent to "Old Comrades" and, as they passed us, really opened up in an irreverent way as they headed in the direction of the Cathedral.

The first of the five tableaux then followed sedately although the horses clattered and strained as they were negotiated up the extra slope of the corner. This Whit Monday of 1926 coincided with Empire Day and, of course, there could be no other choice for the theme than 'The Empire'. This offered much scope and as they passed the scenes illustrated in turn 'The Discovery of Newfoundland', 'Clive and India', 'Wolfe and the Taking of Quebec', 'Captain Cook in Australia' and finally 'Cecil Rhodes of South Africa'. Also to celebrate, on this particular occasion, the full band of the Second Battalion, The East Yorkshire Regiment had been engaged.

With the hearts of spectators already stirred by thoughts and pride of the Empire, misty eyes greeted the rousing martial sound and the immaculate well drilled bearing of this military band as it marched by in perfect unison. To take a further pull on the heart strings, for the war had not been over all that long, they were playing "It's a long way to Tipperary" and as they came round the Close corner they did so with an accurate wheeling movement which raised a spontaneous outburst of applause.

Following closely on was the civic and official parties sitting in open landaus and holding up white gloved hands in dignified waves yet unable to resist an exchange of words with those they knew in the watching crowd. Attached to these parties, sometimes flanking the Mayor's vehicle as a bodyguard, would be the parade and view of the 'Men at Armes'. About a dozen local youths marched, or rather trudged, along attired in heavy, clinging and uncomfortable suits of chain armour. These were the original suits of the men at arms and were so small that only youths could climb into them. In addition they carried tall pikes and helmets were clamped down over their heads. The weight of all these things together with stiff leather boots of the wrong size were the cause of their trudging and they could hardly be expected to stamp along to the beat of the band. It is sad that these suits, with age and use, have deteriorated to the extent they have fallen apart and cannot now be a feature of the procession.

Eventually came the finale in the form of the local fire brigade, the quietness of their motors being in sharp contrast to the sound of the band just ahead. Then suddenly the centre of the street, clear a moment ago, became a mass of people milling about without, it seemed, intent or direction yet, just as quickly, they formed into well regulated streams through to the entrances to the Recreation Grounds where the Athletic Sports and Cycle Meeting was to take place in the afternoon.

With a last glance along the street we turned and walked briskly home to have a quick meal. We would all be attending the sports, mother as a volunteer in the Tea Tent, ourselves as spectators and we would have to be down there early for father to take us into our seats in the reserved enclosure.

* * * *

Bower Steeplechase, 1924, in Baker's Lane

Press cutting

Bandstand (now demolished), Recreation Ground

The Athletic Sports and Cycle Meeting had been a traditional event since before the turn of the century and my father, as a young man, had taken part successfully. The racing track was just beyond the main ornamental grounds on extensive flat ground overlooked by the park of Beacon House. The track itself was in the shape of an egg to fit into the confines of the field itself and, because of the space available, spectators to a depth of eight or nine could be accommodated. Along the straight nearest the entrance, at this time, stood a pleasant ornamental bandstand of cast iron and it was here that we listened to many concerts by the City and visiting bands on Sunday evenings. Curiously, also near the racing track is a larger than life size bronze statue of Commander Edward John Smith, captain of the ill-fated Titanic and who went down with her in April, 1912. Captain Smith was born in Hanley yet the statue was erected, for some very obscure reason, in Lichfield. Another curious aspect of the memorial is that the inscription made no mention of the Titanic and this had to be added in May, 1985. But the crowds would not care about Captain Smith at this particular time as they would be concentrating on obtaining a good position at the side of the race track.

Father would arrange for my brother and I to go in at the committee entrance and from where we would be elevated to the privileged enclosure by the winning post. At this point, some distance back from it, was a gardener's cottage, part of which, for the purpose of the athletics, was set up as a First Aid post. Spills on the track were numerous and during the course of the afternoon we would watch, with rather a morbid interest, the casualties as they were carried past us for remedial measures which appeared to consist only of white bandages and liberal applications of iodine. But such diversions were incidental to our intense interest in the racing. We thoroughly enjoyed ourselves and studied the programme in detail looking for the names of local competitors and, for some reason unknown, those who were members of the Birchfield Harriers Club. I think they ran in black vests with a stag on the chest.

Until a few years earlier the cycle track had been grass and, looking back now, it could hardly have been satisfactory. The effort needed to obtain racing speed demanded so much more physical effort. Furthermore, any moisture on the grass would cause greasiness and, therefore, danger with ruts forming as the afternoon ran on. And, of course, at the curved ends there was no banking which caused further hazards, although if there was a spill, turf was much less hurtful to the knees and elbows.

When we started seriously to follow the racing the City Council had constructed a fine red cinder track with banking at each end. The banking at the sharp end was rather steep and, we assumed from complaints we overheard, rather dangerous. But the sport was improved considerably and the races much faster which, in turn, caused more spills and the traffic on its way past us to the first aid room, increased both in numbers and in the more lurid nature of the injury for there was, now, a mixture of gravel and blood. Protective head gear was not compulsory at this time!

I think the "devil take the hindmost" races were the most interesting to us although we had some difficulty in working out what was going on. We always made a note of the scratch rider, usually Harry Genders, in a handicap and great was our joy if he managed to creep through the field to win in the last few yards — heads well down into the handle bars, straining on the pedals with the front wheels swaying and jerking alarmingly as they reached the line. It always amused us when the leading cyclist, instead of turning his head to check his position, would dip his head and look back under his saddle to obtain the required information.

The running events were held on the grass in the middle of the track and we took less interest in them than the cycling, although again we were careful to note if there were any local runners.

Towards the end of the afternoon sitting there, under the scorching sun and becoming rather hungry, and certainly very thirsty, we forsook the last few races and went off in search of mother in the Tea Tent. The Tea Tent was a huge affair with a very long counter erected specially on the ornamental lawns near the museum building. The ladies of the Tea Committee had taken on an entirely voluntary service to provide sufficient cups of tea and refreshments to satisfy the hundreds of people in the recreation grounds on a Whit Monday afternoon. All the ladies, including mother, were run off their feet in their attempts to dispense the refreshments, but they stuck to their task and there were few complaints. Mother soon supplied us with a bun and a bottle of pop. Our throats were so parched that fizzy pop was pure nectar as we gulped it down straight from the bottles with the glass marbles rattling against the side. We would then hang about the tent for a while until mother was ready to walk back home. The clearing up was generally left until the next day. On our way home we would discuss the various items of the procession and, more often than not, father would catch us up after finishing his duties at the sports and everyone would settle down for a quiet hour in the coolness of the rooms at home.

* * * *

But Bower day was by no means over for we would all set out later in the evening to walk around the fair and amusements. Curiously, on this visit, we seldom went on any of the roundabouts or other machines. It was in later years that we started throwing darts or partaking in the cocoanut shies. We were content now to have the fun of watching. It amused us to see 'all the fun of the fair'. The shouts of the stallholders, the laughter of the crowds, the 'find the lady' tricksters, the patter of the cheap jacks and, all the time, the fair organ whirling through the popular tunes.

Wandering up to Greenhill we always made an annual visit to a small sweet shop on the corner of Gresley Row opposite the Holly Bush Inn. Here Mrs. Hackett expected us for we never called at any other time and she was able to express surprise as to how we were growing. Meanwhile, her son, helping behind the counter, was providing us with bags of brandy snaps which we quickly broke off into pieces before devouring. The son had bright red hair, greased back, and he was, in his spare time, the second eleven umpire.

But we would not leave Greenhill yet because here were the larger side-shows and we asked if we could see the lion faced lady and other freaks and the 'Wall of Death' which swayed about frighteningly as we gazed down from a position high up over the crowds. The wall of death became more horrific each year with the solo motor cyclist whooshing round inside and introducing further allegedly death defying stunts, finishing up one year with a tiger on the pillion seat!

Illuminations, Minster Pool

Margaret, 1932

Myself, 1932

Gettler's Shop, Tamworth Street.

Tamworth Street.
Gettlers Shop Name Sign left hand middle.

The public houses had been open all through the day and by the time we were ready to make for home more than one person would be lurching about rather inebriated. As we made our way for Beacon Street we would pass by Minster Pool, the waters shimmering against lights at the far end in Dam Street. These lights prompted our parents to recall how, near the turn of the century and again before the war, all the trees and edges of the pool had been decorated with fairly lights and a party of glee singers from the Cathedral Choir sang across the water from a lighted craft. They told us how wonderful this fairyland scene was and father said how much he would like it to be repeated. He had his wish but had to wait until 1935 on the occasion of George V's Jubilee when the lights appeared again and the strains of "just a song at twilight" floated in the evening air.

As we walked on the sounds from the fair organ were still rendering "Over the Waves" to the night sky and we could hear shouts and screams as people on the swings reached their full precarious heights.

Mother often told us in later years how father, having had his supper and discussed the day with her, would go outside into the front garden and look towards the silhouettes of the spires of the Cathedral with the lights of the town still glowing slightly. All, by then, would be quiet and quite peaceful and he would, without fail, turn to mother, put his arm around her shoulder and say "the Bower is over, Lichfield sleeps". As we grew on we ourselves would inherit this ritual and on many other nights, in the quietness, we would look down to the Spires and quote "Lichfield sleeps".

* * * *

But, of course, as the years passed the Bower started to take, for us, a different aspect. We attended it on our own and found ourselves showing some skill with the darts, shooting accurately the plumed air gun pellets and, using our cricket ball throwing ability, to hurl the cocoanuts to the ground with some regularity, although the lightness of the wooden balls provided tended to suggest our throwing arm could leave its socket. Of course, we found other reasons for showing off on the swings and the dodgem cars. The fair sex seemed pleased when we dared to support them protectively on the flying roundabouts and the big wheels. It was at a Bower evening such as this that I first met Margaret. Not that it was entirely by chance because we both knew some conspiracies were afoot between our friends and we, ourselves, had stolen smiles across the aisle during the sermon at St. Michael's Church despite the surveillance of our respective families sitting with us. But here we were, suddenly face to face, along Tamworth Street, outside Gettlers shop, amongst the swirling crowds of the Bower. We stood there unaware that our friends had discreetly drifted away. We had dared to stop and were there together. Margaret, demure, slightly freckled and lovely; myself, something of an awkward and gawky grammar school boy, now suddenly shy and not knowing exactly what to say.

There are few, if any, moments in a lifetime such as this: two young people meeting for the first time and realising that both are so pleased and delighted to be together. So we, too, swirled off into the Bower on to the merry-go-rounds and the swings and through the dark tunnels of the ghost train.

We would eventually leave the Bower and walk together, slowly, along Church Street towards Margaret's home down at Wissage where, at the garden gate by the apple orchard, we would pause and talk for awhile and say goodnight in a hesitant sort of way. Days later I would cycle back to Wissage and walk with Margaret along the lane near her home and a single kiss, by the little gate into Scotch Orchard, sealed our fate and our happiness. As we walked back we were not aware of the drizzle of rain and the mist clouds forming low across the late spring fields for, to us, the sky above was blue and wide, an unseen lark carolled high above and harmonised the joy we had in our young hearts. We are still lucky to have that same blue sky today (albeit a Warwickshire one) and hear that unseen lark still singing above some fifty and more years on.

* * * *

The same traditional magic of the Bower continued but in a changed way. The cycle meetings eventually lost their attraction and we boys found ourselves playing in all day matches up at the cricket field but, nevertheless, well satisfied that stumps would be drawn in time for us to trail off down to the Bower and go on everything and act the goat on the Cake Walk.

Inevitably, as time flies by, exile from the Greenhill Bower comes along and, on a Whit Monday now, I can only stare across a different garden and from there, with Margaret, relive the Bower days that were, and then in the twilight, look across the sky to the north west, visualise the Spires and wonder whether "the Bower is over" and whether "Lichfield sleeps".

Chapter Eight

GRAMMAR SCHOOL

I suppose I was one of those unusual, perhaps curious, individuals who enjoyed every moment of my years at school and look back on them with happiness and pleasure. Before going to the Grammar School I attended three other local schools.

The first, the infants school in Beacon Street just a stones throw from home. I was well acquainted with this school for my Aunt Annie George, who lived near us, had been headmistress there for many years before she transferred to Elmhurst Village School to which she cycled some three miles every day. Miss Enstone had succeeded her and I remember her to be very kind but my only memento from the school was a small bag which I had threaded on a card with raffia.

I transferred from here to Christ Church School a mile away across the fields by which way I walked with a group of other children from Beacon Street each day. I enjoyed this school and received a good grounding, especially of the multiplication tables which we monotonously chanted out over and over again for Miss Catherwood to the extent that Miss Wootton and the headmaster, Mr. Cooper, in the classrooms on either side had, eventually, to complain. It was in this class that, turning forward the pages of the history book, I was fascinated by a picture of Napoleon riding a white horse. I looked forward to the lesson in which we would learn about him. But alas, I was ill at that specific time and missed the lesson, but settled later for Nelson's chapter and he became my hero from that time. Miss Moss was the teacher in the fourth class, she had bright ginger hair and rimless spectacles which tended to belie her kindness and emphasise sterness. It was from her class that I obtained my minor C Scholarship for the Grammar School entrance. The headmaster, Mr. H. L. Cooper, followed my career throughout and many years later, was sending congratulatory postcards about professional appointments and, even, deeds on the cricket field.

I passed on to the Central School which was then in Frog Lane. Frog Lane University we called it. I remember well the friendliness of the teachers there; Mr. Pullen and Miss Baker and the head, Mr. Roberts. But I was only there a few months and as my brothers were already attending the Grammar School I could not wait to get there.

When first I attended in 1925 there were less than 130 pupils and everyone knew the other. There were eight forms with a corresponding number of masters. In addition to these forms were the Big School, common rooms for masters and prefects and dormitories and other rooms for the boarders, much as is usual in most grammar schools of that time. My two brothers were well established and I became "Brown III". My eldest brother, when he first attended was, apparently, quite a small boy, so much so that he was christened "Spot". As was the custom this nickname was also handed down and I duly became "Spot III". When my elder brother left I was reduced to "Spot II" and so on. But the name remained all through school life and, to some, long after.

The same masters, with few exceptions, remained all through my school career and, with the school being so small, we had a very happy relationship with them and they showed a fine sense of humour when the occasion demanded. Later when they joined in games of rugger the division disappeared further for the middle of the scrum is common ground. But we did not take advantage of this position and, because of our respect for them, discipline was adequately maintained. Many times have I caught a master's eye and read a half hidden smile which satisfied me they were still quite young at heart with us. When knocking at their study door with some message one was greeted with a room of black gowned figures in varying stages of recline and the atmosphere across the room a complete fog of tobacco smoke so dense that it was almost impossible to make out the pictures hanging on the wall. After the bell they brought a whiff of this atmosphere with them in the classroom.

The school facade was built on classical lines with one three storey block from which stretched out the Big School, with the boarders dormitories above, along to the ivy clad walls of the headmaster's house. This main block was considerably lower than the playing fields with a drive to them so steep that once the driver of a four wheeled horse dray, fully laden with coal, under-estimated it and gradually the load over-powered the horse and pulled him backwards in a somersault. A quick knot of boys collected to see the horse lying between the shafts but making sure they were clear of some flaying hooves. In spite of the panic someone remembered to ring the bell and after school every-thing had been restored to normal.

At the top of this drive, approached by steps, was a long, old army hut which was divided into three classrooms. Those attending school at this time will have pleasant memories of the huts, affectionately called A, B and C. Hut C was on ground level but the slope of the field was such that Hut A was some three to four feet aboveground and access gained by four wooden steps. The intervening space harboured all sorts of flotsam from goal posts to corner flags, rolls of wire netting to garden tools and, as the headmaster's fowls lived in the near vicinity, lessons were frequently accompanied by the clucking of hens, sheltering or having a dust bath.

Another feature of the huts was that they were heated by a system of coke stoves which, to say the least, were abysmally inefficient and the whole issue likely to go up in flames. In the winter quite a number of lessons had to be abandoned through lack of heat and the ink wells had usually frozen solid. We did not mind for we were let out on to the adjacent playing field where a game of football was quickly organised between the day boys and the boarders.

The far hut, C, was where I started in form two. The form master was pleasant and he liked to crack a joke but we always suspected his mind tended to wander to the amateur dramatics upon which he was so keen. His discipline, perhaps of all the masters except woodwork, left something to be desired and, at times, there was bedlam in his class with one fellow actually standing up and reciting, quite loudly, a very shady ditty from start to finish.

The middle hut, or B, was generally the maths room, although the History and English teacher occasionally found himself in it. At the other extremity hut A was the domain of the deputy head, the French master. He allowed no other master to use the hut. He was known as 'Sparrow' because he was the officer commanding the Cadet Force and when attired in his khaki breeches and

Early Beacon Street Infants School

Lichfield Grammar School and playing fields

Grammar School Staff, 1929

J. R. Lindley, P. Laithwaite, E. J. Ball, Revd. R. W. Clarke, A. L. Harding, R. H. Jacob, H. T. W. Peach.

puttees his legs looked particularly thin — hence the sparrow association.

The corps was a voluntary part of school life and was usually held in the last period of a Friday afternoon. It covered the basis of a military training, arms drill, marching, signalling and the like. Presumably someone in the War Office had co-operated with the Education Authorities to organise it with the obvious reason that boys, having had military training, would find it useful in case another war flared up.

We were issued with regulation khaki uniforms. The caps were of the officer peaked type with the Staffordshire knot of the South Staffs Regiment on the cap badge. For some peculiar reason we were not issued with, nor allowed to wear, long trousers but had to put up with short ones with puttees encasing our legs over the stockings. Puttees were not the easiest apparel to put on but eventually we acquired the knack and were able to walk about without them slipping down. Each Thursday evening, in term time, found us complete with tins of Brasso and button sticks, polishing our buttons, cap badges and other accoutrements for parades the next afternoon. On parade we would 'order arms', 'slope arms', 'present arms' and any other movement involving a rifle and march over the playing fields wheeling and halting and forming columns of fours. All the commands would be bawled at us by the sergeant standing near the cricket pavilion with 'Sparrow' in close supervisory presence. Once out of ordinary earshot we felt free to carry on our banter and laugh at jokes from the rear ranks, but as the sergeant managed to direct us towards him, like the fetch at a sheep dog trial, we were, once again, an innocent, quiet, squad of cadets. I volunteered the join the signalling unit but as I could never really master the morse code I had some difficulty in deciphering messages flagged over from the other side of the field, or even from the top of adjacent Borrowcop Hill and the countryside beyond. If only they had flagged a little slower I might have picked up a message accurately. But it was pleasant to feel the flag taken up in a breeze and to hear the flapping noise as we signalled the short ones and the long ones of the morse code.

Each year we were offered the opportunity of attending a Cadet Camp, usually in the vicinity of a holiday resort. The first one I attended was spread out on the sea flats, now a golf course I believe, under the Conway mountains in North Wales where we were under canvas and I do not have particularly warm recollections of it. Rolling up the skirts of a bell tent, at seven o'clock in the morning, to admit a cold and damp sea breeze was not my usual lifestyle at that early hour. Other camps at Deal and Cowes took place in well built huts which were truly rather more amenable. The camp at Cowes usually coincided with Cowes Regatta week and after a morning of parades we were free to attend the sights. I well remember George V coming ashore on one occasion from one of his smaller yachts. But, otherwise we could never understand the comings and goings of the yacht races nor the gun shots which controlled them.

Even at a camp such as this we could have miserable moments. I can think of nothing more miserable than the guard duty which we had, in turn, to undertake. I arranged to do my duty with Dennis but after the initial fascination and a giggle we found ourselves, well before the dawn, cold, tired and possibly home sick and wondering what on earth we were doing there at all. Matters were not helped by the duty sergeant changing guard, not outside with us using smart staccato commands, but from the warmth of his truckle bed with a sleepy wave of the arm.

* * * *

In 1933 the old huts were abandoned and re-sited further over the playing fields, making space for the erection of a complete new wing of classrooms and a gymnasium. Prior to this our other main classrooms had been contained in the three story block of the main school with the chemistry lab on the top floor, presumably, in case anyone became too enthusiastic with a test tube and blew the place up.

One of my greatest experiences had happened in the geography room just below. Morning class was being conducted quite normally when suddenly our attention was called to a babble of voices gathering on the gravel beneath the window. We all looked up and shot questionning glances across to each other and the Master, also mystified, walked to the window and said "Look, look", and as we all stood up and looked out there, to the south east in the sky was what appeared to be an immense grey orb. It looked large and unreal. "The R.101" someone shouted and, with one accord, we charged out of the room and joined the rest of the boys, now assembling on the playing field. With graceful splendour the airship approached, quite rapidly, although its size belied its speed. The initial circular appearance was changed as the full length of her structure came over us. It was quite low and one of the most impressive and thrilling sights I have ever seen. The gigantic airship gleamed as it approached across the sky and as it flew even nearer we were able, clearly, to discern the tiny gondalas, at least they looked tiny in comparison to the main bulk. We could see faint dark trails of smoke and, with it came the beautiful pulsating music of the great diesel engines. Up there in a clear sky it seemed to glide along so easily almost as if on a breeze and as it drew immediately overhead we could read the lettering in black G.FAAW and R.101 flanking to the rear. Someone raised a cheer and I am sure, at that moment, every schoolboy standing there was overcome almost to tears with wonder and pride.

But the great ship flew on and it disappeared gradually over Cherry Orchard yet everyone lingered on, unable to tear eyes away from the lessening shape. A schoolboys love of an airship was natural but to have actually seen one passing overhead and so low was the experience of a lifetime. Eventually we retraced our steps to the classrooms, but we were unable to settle down and were in no mood to study the geography of the world — our world, at that moment, was the dirigible in the sky just over the horizon. Small wonder then, the horror which struck us when we awoke one October Sunday morning a year later to learn that the R.101 had crashed in a field near Beauvais in France during a thunderstorm. This was disaster indeed.

* * * *

The anatomy of most schools includes a quadrangle. Ours was quite large and had the physics laboratory flanking it on one side and, on the other, a very long bicycle shed which, on most days, was full to overflowing. Behind this, and

Grammar School Boys

The R.101 approaching Lichfield, October 1929

Photograph by Courtesy Lichfield City Council

just over a hawthorn hedge was the woodwork shop. Here we could relax and, incidently, have fun. We would construct our eggstands, book ends and little bits of furniture each with the appropriate shell transfer placed thereon and take them all proudly home to our mothers. But, regretfully, the main attraction was the complete lack of discipline throughout the lesson. In the middle of an explanation of the construction of a dovetail joint a wooden block missile would be launched from a position near the door and it would hurtle across the benches and, having missed the intended target, finish up against the corrugated iron wall with a resounding zoink. Taking not the slightest notice the woodwork master would bend down, unloosen the vice and continue his almost inaudible discourse. Meanwhile, at the far end, ammunition for a retaliatory broadside was being sought from amidst the sawdust and shavings on the floor.

* * * *

Across at the main school all would be bustle. The corridor outside the common rooms would be agog with boys moving in all directions. Space was limited. It took an effort to make a way to the notice boards, let alone stand long enough to see if you were picked for next Wednesday's practice game, or worse, whether you were in detention. Of the two notice boards the larger was for general school matters and the other, on the opposite wall was divided into four for House notices. The Houses had been chosen from nationally famous Lichfeldians and the name of each with its appropriate colour was emblazoned at the top. Written threats and taunts usually adorned each notice. Addison (yellow) would be referred to as Addled Addison, Garrick (blue) as Greasey Garrick, Johnson (green) as Jammy Johnson and the boarders house Darwin (red) as Dirty Darwin. It can be deduced that house rivalry was intense at all levels particularly where games were concerned. Knowing this someone had been most politic to ensure that John, Dennis and myself were placed in the same House — Johnson.

Just on hand were the locker rooms with hand basins and toilets close by. Each boy had a locker to himself and a suitable key — which we were always losing. The doors of the lockers were hinged at the top and we stood with our head under the door holding it up. The difficulty arose when the person either above or below wished to get to his locker at the same time. As your status rose in the school so you were promoted to a better locker until, at last, when as a sixth former and a prefect, a large side hinged locker was allocated.

A corridor connected all these ancilliary precincts to the hub of the whole establishment, the Big School. It was a large well lit room with a stage and a desk for the head. Assembly was held here and, unfortunately, the long ten foot desks faced to the front and thus, if late, there was no chance of just slipping in at the back and you either hung about or faced the full limelight of walking in late. I only just made it on many occasions.

* * * *

But really the central character of our whole school life was the headmaster, the Reverend R. W. Clarke, M.A. Indeed, he was the school: it was he who set the high standard of learning and the very high standard of behaviour, both within the school bounds and in the streets outside. Severe and menacing though he was we all loved him.

He was really a most unbelievable fellow. To us he always appeared to be old, certainly he was rather deaf, but there were times when he appeared not to be. He was stockily built with a head sunk well in his shoulders and it was these features which awarded him the nickname of "Hippo". He wore a smart, well-cut, clerical grey suit with a snow white dog collar and always the most highly polished black shoes. No boy who attended this school during his reign could ever possibly forget him, yet all held him in a mixture of awe, fear and respect. He ruled with a rod of iron and a five foot cane. Sometimes, even in class, he seemed to be in a world of his own and quite oblivious to the boys quaking before him. Yet he was human, for when his wife called for him from the nether regions of their quarters he would, whatever he had been doing, charge down Big School, sleeves of his gown flowing behind and continually repeating "Coming my dear, coming" and as he disappeared the double swing doors leading to his domain were heard to swing and flap as he swept through them. We usually knew when he was coming back because the flapping of the doors was repeated in reverse and his approach would be broadcast without the need to station a lookout.

The flowing sleeves of his gown were significant because therein he housed his five foot cane. Woe betide the unfortunate individual who had transgressed sufficiently to receive a sentence of six of the best. Luckily I was never such a recipient but I have witnessed, with horror, trepidation and sympathy, the theatre of such a thrashing and felt very thankful that I was not the one going through it.

The ceremony would take place on the stage in front of the whole school. The victim would make his way up where, with a most severe expression, Hippo would denounce the extent of the misdemeanour of which the poor fellow had been found guilty. Having pulled the cane out of his sleeve, like a sword from its scabbard, the audience gasped in breathless anticipation, the boy would be instructed to hold out his hand. He would have decided previously whether he held out his right or his left hand. I would have held out my left hand, having in mind I was right handed. There then followed something of a cat and mouse game. Hippo would measure the distance and raise his cane to take careful aim and the boy would measure his distance so that he could lower his hand at the moment of impact and thus take out some of the sting. Anyway the first stroke came down with a swish and the boy at the last moment withdrew his hand making the cane miss and strike the floor. A snigger rippled across the back few rows, but either Hippo did not hear or he chose to ignore it, so intent was he on the matter in hand. He quickly positioned himself for the second blow and it landed on target with an awful thwack. For the next three swings honours were even, the boy judging his hand movement better with practice. Eventually Hippo returned grim faced and breathless to his desk and the boy receded back to his form room mates holding his hand between body and arm. I always suspected a look of triumph on his face — not tears. I am sure, had it been allowed, he would have received a generous round of applause.

But this performance could be completely upstaged if it was a bend over situation. This almost reached farcical proportions. The same mutual sparring

The Reverend R. W. Clarke, M.A.

School First Fifteen 1933
Myself 2nd from right next to Dennis (Captain)

would take place but in this instance the boy was at a complete disadvantage because, bending over, he was unable to see the cane and judge the blow. On the other hand Hippo would have a much larger target to aim at, a target inflated by the thickness of newspapers stuffed down the trousers. This unreal shape of the posterior, although quite obvious to the spectators, was entirely lost on the head who, in his apparent rage, would miss such niceties of shape and, merely instructing the boy to 'bend tighter', would start the onslaught. This appeared to be of such ferocity that gasps again went up and down the hall. Then, after the first few exploratory blows, Hippo threw all caution to the winds and lost all sense of direction.

Now Big School was lighted by gas brackets extending down from the ceiling and branched into two arms with globes at the end of each. Those arms over the stage would, thus, be nearer to the floor. Consequently it was inevitable that in the flurry of wild swipes the cane, at some time, would get mixed up with the gas brackets. His final swings had unerring aim on that bracket which swung like a pendulum. Hippo snorted back to his desk as if nothing had happened. But the boy was not quite sure whether or not it was all over because he would not have known whether the hits on the bracket had been registered for or against him.

It was performances such as this which struck fear into our hearts and deterred us from straying into misdemeanours that would warrant being "sent to the head". There have been occasions when boys being "sent" have disappeared in the direction of the head's study, hung about the boarders' common room for about five minutes and re-appeared to re-join his form room. I shudder to contemplate the consequences of such action had the head learned of this ruse.

These occasions did not happen all that often but when they did they always struck home forcibly and there must have been a firm resolve not to allow oneself to succumb to ill deeds. It was certainly a deterrent. It was this awe with which the head was held that gave him so much authority to keep the school under control. Yet I doubt if the 'crime' ever justified such severe punishment because the individual himself approached the ordeal, not with humiliation, but with some bravado and a determination to put up a brave show and not let his friends down.

Even in class "Hippo" had his peculiarities. He taught Latin. His method was unfortunate, to say the least. He would take a class of some 20 boys in a room that could hold over a hundred. We sat on the extremities of long desks set in rows, either side of the central gangway. The idea was that you could not work in collusion or even carry on a conversation. But the head was allegedly deaf and so we were able to talk out quite loudly and freely to each other. But you had to be careful. Thus, when we had a test those who knew the answers shouted them out. But we had to be sure the correct answers were given or else it would have looked suspicious. He would sit up at his desk talking some fifteen yards away from his nearest pupil. We never had the chance to ask him to repeat or explain anything. Occasionally he would resort to the blackboard but this would only increase the conversation behind him. However, on occasions he would suddenly hold out his arm behind his back and pointing his finger in a general direction would say "stop talking down there". Apparently he had some weird method of looking at a reflection in his pince nez spectacles.

On other occasions he would suddenly stop, his face would flush and his eyes go beady as he glared somewhere into the Big School. Silence — then, after awhile a sudden shout apparently in anger "you boy, stand up" and he would again point in a general direction. This caused something of a dilemma as we had all been talking and would not know to whom he was referring. There was no point standing up if it was not you. We could not last out forever and someone, at the front, would stand up. "No., no, not you" and the boy behind would stand up: "no, no, not you" and in turn the next would stand. Eventually the boy at the back, after a glance behind, would be left standing isolated and would have to take the full force of the reprimand. It was at such moments as this you hoped his wife would call him to the phone because, when he came back, he would have forgotten all about it.

I well remember one lunchtime. It must have been raining for practically the whole school was congregated in the Big School shouting, throwing a ball, climbing desks and ragging about generally. The door had opened slowly and silently and from it came the most horrendous and extended bellow. It emanated from the Head standing in the doorway. A fearful silence descended over the room but worse, far worse we thought, for as he stood there with everyone frozen, a tennis ball rolled slowly out from under a desk. His eyes fell from boy level down to the floor and to the ball as it came to rest against the wall. The dreadful silence continued and those nearest to him and to the ball may well have offered up a prayer. Then he suddenly opened up and for fully two minutes roared out a lecture on correct and decent behaviour, the proper way to treat other people's furniture, that playing fields were provided at great expense for ball games and expanded on the worthless creatures we were. With bated breath we waited for the tirade to subside and for the passing of sentence. When suddenly, someone outside, unaware of the drama going on within, rang the bell for afternoon school and thus certainly saved our situation. And so we got away with it but not without final dire threats should such bedlam disturb his lunch again.

Such lectures, when they came, contained a queer mixture of threat and advice but, of course, he was right and his disciplinary code was all to our good. He would not have us seen in the town without our caps. He would not have us eating in the street under any circumstances and we always had to be aware our appearance befitted the school and our homes. He was not going to have us, as he put it, 'looking like wire haired terriers'. Why this particular breed was singled out was never explained.

He was a great sportsman and encouraged us on all fields of play. But even here he had his set rules from which he could not divert. In cricket, to him, the first run must be run as quickly as possible. During one school match I played for a single to give my brother the bowling and I was able to stroll to the other end. But this was not approved by the head who jumped out of his deckchair on his lawn with a loud instruction to "run it quicker boy!" It was he who, with other masters, ensured the changing of the school game from soccer to rugby. He had played and knew the game well. Time upon time he would appear during a match and, irrespective of the position of the game, would come out shouting "go low, go low". On any particularly dry day he insisted that we soaked the leather ball in a bucket of water which, he rightly said, made handling of the ball so much more sure.

He kept a strict eye on athletics too and, insisted that we always dressed properly for the occasion. These times were before the introduction of track suits and on one sports day I remember a member of our house kept his flannel trousers on over his running shorts. He took them off at the starting line in full view of parents and sisters alike. At the following Monday morning assembly "Hippo" lectured about this embarrasing act and required us, in future, to show more modesty in front of parents and the fair sex.

All athletes were included in his rigid code of standards and I am sure he would have banned completely any of us who might have dared to introduce the Fossbury Flop. That would have been too much!

But in spite of all these things we fully respected him, his discipline and his high standards. We realised the school would not have been as good had he not been there, and we also knew if there was any chance of asking a dignatory for a half days holiday "Hippo" would be the first to get one for us.

* * * *

I took full advantage of opportunities for playing games at school which was not surprising as my father, sister and elder brother were already so keen in their sporting spheres. Encouragement from the then games master, Mr. Jacob, we called him "Cheesey", was an added incentive. Games were played on Wednesday and Saturday afternoons in term time for we had school on Saturday mornings.

In the summer there would be three or four games of cricket going on at the same time and square leg in one match would overlap cover point in another. Masters would umpire at both ends and make the bowling changes. Gradually stature grew as runs were made and we soon found ourselves in the school second eleven playing against the other grammar schools in the area. My brother and I had an added advantage that, from a young age, we attended the local club matches where father was captain of the second XI. For many years, whenever possible, we had been scorers and, obviously, if one of the team failed to turn up we were pitchforked into the eleven. In due course we found ourselves fully fledged members of the School First XI.

Here again the Head's keenness came to the fore for he had always offered to give a bat to boys making a fifty. John had earlier achieved this mark and we, in turn, made a number of fifties. So much so that the head, realising we would not wish to make a collection of bats, adjusted his offer to pads, gloves and cricket bags. We were thus set up for our cricketing careers beyond school.

We achieved the same status on the rugger field where we worked our way up through the ranks of the house matches to the First XV. Here again the advantage of always playing with a brother was manifest and the intimacy with which we knew each other's movements paid dividends. But let it be said we were only individual members of the teams and the team spirit and the laughs and the banter were all part of being successful.

During the Easter term we turned to athletics which started with cross-country practice and training runs. These were undertaken at least two or three afternoons in the week which included paper chases. I am sure public indignation of handfuls of paper being thrown about the countryside brought an abandonment to this variation of running.

On these runs I never ran until I dropped and I am sure my father's "little bit extra" did not involve falling to the ground at the post and staying there flat out for half an hour or so. Although we ran for our house over all, an accumulation of individual points qualified you to be a recipient of a silver cup. As I write I glance at four of them now on the shelf at my side. Bright talismen and reminders of days in the sun when there were no aches or pains, when the air rippled on supple muscles running hard for the tape and when life was young.

*   *   *   *

As with all schools one of the most important, if not the most important, quarter was the Tuck Shop. We had one in the form of a private sweet shop situated, luckily, right at the entrance to the school drive. Thus it could be considered legitimate and not out of bounds to nip down the drive and into the shop. It was run by one Miss Barker who was really a kind old soul but she had to put up with so much banter and leg pulling that she always had to be on her guard and, should the occasion arise, she could really be quite sharp and irate. Mother always called in after speech and sports days and became quite fond of her. Years after leaving school old boys generally called in to pay their respects and, I have no doubt, she would always remember their names and recall some incident relating to them. I know that years after I left she still referred to me as Spot III.

In the early days the shop was very small, dark and badly arranged. So much so that there was little room for display and most commodities were sold direct from the cardboard boxes they came in. Wire trays of buns, doughnuts and the like remained unsorted and exposed on top of the counter and they were frequently sent flying when we all crowded into the limited space at 'break'. In due course they would be retrieved, some from the floor, possibly wiped and quickly sold to unsuspecting latecomers. But such was the success of business from a guaranteed clientele that one holiday period, unknown to us, she had the whole front area gutted and when we turned up at the start of the next term the whole aspect had been transformed. Not only were our delicacies fully on view but extra space had been allocated for us to mill about and tables and chairs provided in one of her own rooms from which to partake of our lunch. It will be realised that school canteens had not been introduced and day boys staying would congregate here in the Tuck Shop. After the previous confined conditions we felt we now ate in some luxury.

We always stayed on a Monday and our 'meal' was fare purchased over the counter and mother allowed us one shilling for this purpose. This was ample for our needs and consisted of a bottle of pop, a couple of alpines (an iced bun with a central bit of jam), probably a jam doughnut and a large currant bun. As regards the latter, we bit off the side and pressed in a 2d bar of Cadbury's milk chocolate and ate it as a sandwich. It is small wonder that in later years I developed diabetic tendencies. At break we would have already indulged in a tuppeny marshmallow. These were all the rage in vanilla, coffee or strawberry flavour and they were so popular that Miss Barker dispensed many gross during the week.

But we survived — even though many times her cat had to be brushed off the counter where it had settled down for a sleep amongst the alpines.

As I progressed through the school the more I enjoyed it. Perhaps it was because we were so rapidly growing up, the masters recognised this and became closer on a common level. There were discussions on matters unrelated to school. Lessons became so much easier because of it, especially to myself, for at this stage, I was realising the need for learning but even then I found a conflict with my outdoor activities and rather than have my head in a book I would be over at the nets, playing tennis with my brother, or going on long training runs along dark, but well known, country lanes leading from home and, of course, by now I had met Margaret.

I had moved through the school with an air of youthful lightheartedness with my brothers and the same group of friends and, although we recognised the codes of behaviour, were always ready to have fun. This spirit is, perhaps, reflected in two extracts from articles published in school magazines of this period. The first was from a series by a sixth former who we nicknamed 'Sally' and we thought the play on his own nickname and my name, amongst others, was clever.

———— ?

HE that hath a quiet mind and a strong heart showeth great wisdom in that he heareth and believeth, even though with pain, the words which I, Tsa Lee, the chronicler, do speak.

Long ago, ere my beard had shown itself, I discovered, after embarking upon a "Skola" ship, the city of "Ly-chfeeld Skule." In the midst of this most ancient city was a market place which men called "Thekwad." On one side of this meeting place was a roofed portion, and I spake to him that did guide us, and asked him what manner of place it might be. And he answered and said, "It is called the 'By Kshed,' and it is there that the rich keep their chariots."

Now all around us surged a great throng and we did ask the guide who and what they were and he said, "See, ye seekers of wisdom, those two who frisk about with never a care in the world? They are called 'Brou Wun Tu' and 'Co Wulz Tu,' and they are as brothers. See ye also he that has the scented hair and the smiling face. He is called 'Haar Vezt.' The same is a great magician. He it was at the yearly 'soshul' did conjure up sweet musick by drawing the hair of the horse across the intestine of the cat. Such musick as doth make the heart glad and the feet to rejoice.

The second extract is from a further series by the same author who caricatured us all in turn. In this group I was included at number six.

Page Ten — *The Edwardian Magazine*

just changed the labels on our locker doors "—both know " much about most things," but the one does at least wait until you ask him before he tells what he knows—both appear to be good fellows when you know them—one Sixth Former appears to us to be merging this duet into a trio. Key clue—" Panther " is obvious and points to the other.

(v.) A Fifth Former—hands in pockets—good talker—can spoil a good yarn in the telling of it but often doesn't—can catch a pretty slippy train. Key clues—" brolly " and " monocle " give him away immediately, just as " trilby " denotes his friend.

(vi.) Back with the Sixth—we apologize for leaving this person so late—School Prefect—dark hair—centre parting—Rugger and Cricket—a very creditable certificate—never serious except when he's not talking—good beard—often incoherent. Key clue—" Shoot, you fool!"

(vii.) More apologies to the Sixth—School Prefect—tall—good lungs—" Stop talking "—sometimes as incoherent as the above—admirer of Mr. Clapham—Rugger—perhaps too fond of the " children," yet when we consider his impositions, perhaps not—" The School is going to the dogs." Our key clue has misfired—the walking stick has disappeared.

(viii.) Member of the Staff—" laissay allay "—his maps are a byword—capital V for India—never hurries but generally gets there—capable of rather quaintly humorous remarks which come unexpectedly. Key clue—" Will someone lend me a pencil ? "

For our final character we go to IV. c—of small stature—full of " pep "—cheerful—always has a smile from ear to there—everybody likes him (we think so)—we can't say exactly how he makes his impression, but he does, or he wouldn't be here among the celebrities. The key clue gives him away, for appropriately enough his " bike " is a " Sunbeam "

The reference to "shoot you fool" was also an illustration of our silly selves. A cartoon had appeared in one of the Christmas numbers showing an ethereal Elizabethan gentleman standing at the foot of a bed dressed in tights and short bulging pantaloons. A large iron ball at his feet is manacled to his right ankle. A fanatical football supported has been awakened and, still dazed, sits up in bed shouting "shoot you fool!" This phrase became something of a password and we used it on all sorts of occasions.

But with all this fun and happiness we retained our sense of responsibility, became prefects, heads of our houses, captains of the elevens and the fifteens and, tried to uphold the high standards of the school of which we were so proud.

Even so there were heartaches and worries and examinations but we were young and problems, although appearing overwhelming at the time, seemed to recede more quickly then. And how, on Speech Day, our young voices, with one loud accord, rose up and sang out the School Song, 'Vitai Lampada', thumped out on the piano by the maths master, Percy Laithwaite — "There's a breathless hush in the Close tonight" and how we thrilled when The Gatling was jammed and "the voice of a schoolboy" rallied "the ranks".

We would raise three cheers for Sir Percival Heywood or whoever had been presenting the prizes that year and had given us a half holiday and, afterwards, all troop out of Big School, collect satchels out of our lockers for the last time that term, perhaps call in at the Tuck Shop for a Mars Bar, then cycle our way home to start looking forward to Christmas.

VITAI LAMPADA

THERE'S a breathless hush in the Close to-night —
  Ten to make, and the match to win —
A bumping pitch and a blinding light,
  An hour to play and the last man in.
And it's not for the sake of a ribboned coat,
  Or the selfish hope of a season's fame,
But his Captain's hand on his shoulder smote
  "Play up! play up! and play the game!"

The sand of the desert is sodden red, —
  Red with the wreck of a square that broke; —
The Gatling's jammed and the Colonel dead,
  And the regiment blind with dust and smoke.
The river of death has brimmed his banks,
  And England's far, and Honour a name,
But the voice of a schoolboy rallies the ranks:
  "Play up! play up! and play the game!"

This is the word that year by year,
  While in her place the School is set,
Every one of her sons must hear,
  And none that hears it dare forget.
This they all with a joyful mind
  Bear through life like a torch in flame,
And falling fling to the host behind —
  "Play up! play up! and play the game!"

Henry Newbolt.

Chapter Nine

TOWARDS INDEPENDENCE

I left school in January 1934 after fifteen happy years and, with Ena and John having teaching posts and Dennis at university, I found myself the only one left at home. During my last year at school I had, to some extent, back pedalled and had found some difficulty in formulating my career. With my father's connection with law I had almost finalised my papers to enter that profession but, out of the blue it seemed, an opportunity arose to take up 'Articles of Pupilage' (at father's expense) with the City Engineer. I had not relished being tied down to a desk and this career would take me out and about. In addition I had obtained good results at school in drawing and calligraphy so the situation was ideal. The Council were to provide me with a small allowance and, still living at home, I was likely to be quite viable.

This opening altered my outlook immediately because local matters, which had all been taken for granted, took on a different aspect and I was able to examine them from a fresh angle. Beacon Street, for example, had always flooded in certain parts and then I looked on as an amused spectator as the Council foreman of that time always expressed the opinion that the water "was sinkin' rapid". Now I could see the problem involved and the steps being prepared to overcome the flooding. The Museum building, life known, looked permanent and secure, yet I was to learn there was a foundation problem to solve and even the sewage works, out at Curborough, past which I had walked scores of times without hardly a glance, suddenly evolved an interest in the process and odours going on within the the wide entrance gates.

During the very first week in my new career I found myself being rowed across Minster Pool in winter sunshine with both the City and County Engineers to hold a torch for them to crane their necks to inspect and probe underneath the arches holding up Bird Street. Structures which I had not dreamed were there although I had passed over them most days in the last decade. Eventually as we disembarked by the wall of the Garden of Remembrance I realised how pleasant and varied were these aspects of the profession and felt most satisfied. And so it was with all the roads, the bridges, the estates and the buildings together with all the other municipal and engineering matters with which, in the future, I was to become involved.

I looked back at my happy years at school and realised I was entering a new phase of my life which promised to be just as happy.

* * * *

During the course of a Lichfield year many traditional events were held and, still being local, I was able to attend in my revised 'grown up' status. The Old Fair, for instance, held on Shrove Tuesday still filled the Square with fairground amusements yet it was never as extensive, or so popular, as the Bower, although the Mayor and Corporation paid it all due homage and continued to acknowledge the old custom and the Charters with some ceremony at the Guildhall. For myself, I stood at the back, listened to the speeches, sipped my sherry and, after seeing the Mayor have his free ride on the merry-go-round, slipped off home to eat my pancakes alone with my parents. Mother, in past years, had been accustomed to frying them one after another to satisfy four of us and, as she tossed one high into the air to amuse us, she would ask "Who is ready for the next one?"

The Sheriff's Ride is another continuing Council occasion, held traditionally each year in September. The Sheriff holds honorary office only, with little responsibility or authority, but on the day of the ride it is his day alone and takes some precedence over the Mayor. The Sheriff's Ride is a perambulation of the boundaries of the City and because these boundaries do not necessarily follow highways, footways or definite tracks, the route is preferably followed on horseback. For this reason, therefore, one of the qualifications for the position of Sheriff is the ability to ride a horse. Anyone is free to join the Sheriff in this ancient ride and usually he is accompanied by a fine posse of riders. If the Sheriff does not himself ride, a suitable horse-drawn vehicle is used but, of course, by this method much of the route will need to be missed out and a link up has to be made at salient accessible points. I believe, in later years, Land Rovers have frequently come to the aid of the Sheriff of the day.

The first part of the ride is along Beacon Street and we always watched them go by from our front garden. As they approached they gave the appearance of a hunt en route for the meet but pink coats and hounds were missing. Having left Beacon Street into the Cross-in-Hand Lane the company join the boundary at North Lane and proceed on, in a clockwise direction, around the city.

During the course of the day the Sheriff has to halt for refreshment and other urgent matters. One of the most notable such stopping places was Freeford Park where tents were erected to entertain guests for lunch. It was followed by an ad hoc race meeting. It was at such occasions that many of the personalities of the City converged. Characters who were always associated with these, and other similar gatherings and who were always willing to help with the arrangements and ensure the success of the day. Sam Ashley, without fail, would be there dressed in breeches and leggings, large cloth cap — a typical horse man, talking with knowledge on the chances of any horse in any race. He would also be seen, similarly, at the local point to point meeting out at Fradley. Also present would be Bill Coxon (he it was who sang the 'End of a Perfect Day' in the Hopwas Woods) enjoying to the full the fare provided and all aspects of the sport, yet quite a different person when he had to adjust himself to his more staid, sober and dignified duty as mace bearer. Tommy Charrington and many other stalwarts always turned up and were very much permanent parts of the scene. One other such Lichfield personality, Tommy Walmersley, had in the past risen to the exalted position of Mayor and was the head of his own builders firm. There are many stories about him. He would instruct his carpenter —

> "You mek a door"
> "How big shall I make it sir?"
> "You never mind, mek a door, I'll give you the measurements in the mornin'."

On another occasion the same fellow once said to his apprentice:

"I've taught you all I know and now you know nowt".

But the Sheriff's Ride would continue its perambulation and, after a stop for tea on the front lawn of Knowle Farm, finish much where it had started in Beacon Street. Here the Mayor and Corporation would have been waiting for some time to escort the company back to the Guildhall. Eventually they would all process into the town, complete with mace bearers and entourage, at a slow walking pace with the horses, numbers now dwindled, stamping and jigging, impatient at being reined back to such a pace after a brisk gallop over the Pipe Farm fields leading to the Abnalls. For once the City Band would not be in attendance to add their pomp and music to the occasion but individual members of the band, such as Pom Pom Clews, so named for obvious reasons, could not resist standing at the roadside to watch the procession pass by in a strange but dignified silence.

Further toasts and drinks would be available at the Guildhall before final dispersal. I have no doubt many of the horses would be found temporary stabling along at the Old Crown, a few score yards along Bore Street at the corner with Bakers Lane, to enable their owners to enjoy further sustenance after a tiring day in the saddle. The Old Crown Inn, now demolished, was a popular meeting place for farmers coming into the City both on market days and cattle sale days up at Wintertons Yards in Church Street and many would stay on well into the late evening.

It is said that one farmer far gone, was then, regularly, lifted into his float by friends who would lead the horse into the street, point him in the right direction and smack his hind quarters. The horse would then faithfully proceed all the way home with the farmer still sleeping, regardless, on the floor of the float. The route back of some three miles included at least two left hand turns into by-roads which the horse, with so much practice, was able to negotiate and and arrive back quite safely. Here an old retainer would emerge from his bothy after listening patiently for the sounds of the hoof clops, would not only stable the horse but see that the farmer was carried safely into the house and placed on his bed for a good nights sleep and recovery.

* * * *

For some time I had expressed a wish to own a dog but as the other members of the family were not too enthusiastic the matter had been shelved. With the revised circumstances, however, I renewed my wish but was not entirely sure how best to go about it. I imagined some sort of mongrel like Jumble, William's dog. But father, typically, had other ideas and having been working behind the scenes for some time turned up with one unexpectedly. I was punting a rugger ball about on the tennis lawn at the time and turned to find the dog bounding up behind me. He was an obvious thoroughbred — no mongrel for father! A Gordon setter, only a few months old, jet black with a flurry of golden feathering, a loose and silky coat, playful and lively, attractive in every way. I was delighted with him and, as his temperament became so pleasing, he was to give me, and Margaret, many hours of pleasure over the years. He had the habit, and I believe it was a habit peculiar to this breed, of

The Family, 1933

Floods in Beacon Street

Early Guildhall and Municipal Offices (without the Clock)

The Sheriff's Ride in Beacon Street

Sheriffs Ride, Freeford Park. 1935.
W.B.Littler- Sheriff

Myself outside '250' with Tiger Tim

Tiger Tim

pointing his head to the sky, pursing his lips to form a small aperture through which he emitted a long drawn out rumbling woof which endeared us to him and was an indication that he was in need of a walk or, perhaps, something to eat. I soon learned he would require some pretty long walks and that a few hundred yards on a lead would be quite inadequate.

And so another sequence of walks over the local fields commenced. But even this range was quickly extended, especially with the further information gained by new found maps at the Municipal Offices and areas all over the district were explored. Furthermore Margaret's home was some two miles over on the other side of the City and we rarely covered that intervening distance except with the dog.

I originally named him Tiger but this was quickly shortened to Tim. On a walk with us he would race off, nose to ground, quartering thoroughly every field we crossed and, on occasions, would be a mere black speck in the distance picking up scents, chasing plovers endlessly yet, at a whistle, he would come charging back at a terrific gallop and had we not been on the 'qui vive' he might well have knocked us over.

I have often tried to assess the extra miles he ran, with his ranging, over and above the miles we walked in a straighter line. Back at either of our homes he would flop down as if completely exhausted, yet, at the slightest movement in the room, his eyes would open and look about but not raising his head until sure we were about to be on the move again, his tail tapping the floor as indication that he was ready for the off.

We always look back with extreme pleasure to the times we walked into the Staffordshire countryside. In all seasons, in all weathers, across open fields, through the gorse at Pipe Hill, the soft leaved earth under the beech trees in Fisherwick Woods or along the empty lanes of those yester-years. And always at a glance in the direction of the city we would see the three spires standing clear in the landscape. We have looked back at them over at Curborough where we had just walked down from Fradley into a low sunset with a frost stinging against our chins or coming back from Gentleshaw Common after sheltering from a rainstorm, or even when we had slushed our way along the Farewell Lane, deep in snow, and Tim had bounced up to us, surprised at these new conditions, with his muzzle covered in snow where he had tried to eat it.

Perhaps our favourite walk was to cross the fields at the rear of home to Grange Lane by Haldanes House and on by the brickworks and Scarratts Farm along to Sunnyside where we turned right handed for Elmhurst. We named this road the Elmhurst 'High Road' because of the view down below to the north east which stretched across miles of countryside and we could see, we imagined, almost as far as Derbyshire. This road led down to and past one of the lodges of the old demolished Elmhurst Hall, and where we always stopped to gaze through the large white entrance gate because this was one of those dwellings we liked so much. But after some minutes we would have to steal guiltily away when someone came out of a side door into the garden and we would hurry on to catch up with Tim who had been sitting, bolt upright, far ahead, ears cocked, waiting patiently. Then, as we walked on down to Elmhurst village itself, we would start day-dreaming about a place of our own somewhere in the countryside, preferably an old low rambling house with a garden wall and a door through it into a paddock, a well cut lawn up to french windows. Inside a beeswaxed floor and in the far corner a grand piano on which to trip through our duets on long winter evenings.

Elmhurst itself had many pleasant associations. My aunt was headmistress at the small school many years ago and had cycled out each day from Beacon Street. It was also one of the villages where father had taken his concert party and, as we walked by the iron gate leading to the Mission Hall, my mind slipped back to those gatherings, to the song tunes and to village folk laughing away happy evenings.

Just beyond the village, down through the park past the cricket field, was a level crossing with a signal box over the main Euston line north. The track was straight and the trains hereabouts are just getting into their stride after passing through Trent Valley Sstation. For many years we had cycled or walked to this point for engine spotting. This was the same line on which we had seen trains go by at Hademore when we were on our way to Harlaston but now we watched with a more discerning eye and recorded engine class and number. There was also a wonderful curve for watching at Trent Valley Station itself where it appeared, almost, as if a train would head into the platform upon which you were standing. The station was about three miles from Elmhurst crossing and at night, if I happened to be awake, I could lie and hear the distant roar from the train on this stretch and listen as the sound dwindled and died into the distance. I would imagine the ting of the bell in the signal box and the levers going over and I would try to keep awake to hear the next train approaching but the clock over the fields at Christ Church would strike two and I would drop off before the train came along.

But more recently we visited Elmhurst for cricket matches. Even at school we brothers had organised a cricket eleven which we called the Kestrels. With father, three brothers and two cousins living near we immediately had the nucleus of a side and friends from the school or Lichfield elevens mustered to have a most enjoyable time. We played mostly evening matches and toured all the villages in the vicinity. They were, indeed, pleasant yet well fought games. They were not, however, entirely good for our more serious club matches, and we took our chance with the state of the wicket. Usually there were no sight screens and cattle and their belongings had to be moved from the pitch before, and sometimes, during our match. Village partisans enjoyed turning up to watch and their good humoured banter enlivened the proceedings. Once, playing at Lynn, we inveigled the father of one of our main bowlers to umpire and early in the innings he gave one or two decisions against the local batsmen. From then on, almost after every ball bowled, came the cry from the locals "How's that Dad?".

One of the most pleasant grounds upon which we played was at Burntwood where we took on the staff of the hospital. It was a tree lined ground and the wicket was immaculate, with the outfield mown to perfection. Swallows swept across it but a few feet from the surface so much so that our ambition was to catch one as it flew by where we stood in the slips! We never did! Apart from piling plenty of runs against us they had quite a remarkable batsman called Snitch Neville — so called because of his habit of sniffiing as he was about to face up to each ball. But more remarkable was his leg glide which he executed by cocking up his left leg and, somehow, steering the ball between his legs. We called it his half cock shot. Now I would have thought such a shot would have been suicidal, not only in getting himself out but for the possibility of receiving an injury. But it never happened despite our bowlers doing their utmost to hit the target offered on the leg side!

Other grounds were not so ideal and I remember one pitch where, after a heat wave, I was able to stand my bat upright in one of the cracks. Village fast bowlers on their own pitch were generally lethal and sometimes, thinking we had an easy task, we would reverse the batting order and soon be bundled out to defeat. On another occasion brother John, in a match at Brereton, played out the last over enveloped in a swarm of ants while the rest of us watching anxiously in the shadow of the pavilion, shouted encouragement after each ball, quite unaware of the predicament he was facing. Again, whilst on tour in Cornwall, after an early morning start, the home fast bowler appeared, suddenly, as an ethereal figure charging out of a sea mist that was enveloping part of the ground and which made our intention of knocking the ball into the adjacent Atlantic just below the square leg boundary that more difficult.

What memories the game conjures. 'Laughter learnt of friends under an English Heaven', the smell of mown grass in the outfield on a June day, Blancoing our boots and pads the night before, my first catch, long ago, off a skier at fine leg and the pleasure and relief to realise the ball was safely in my hands and my father saying 'Well caught, Cuth', long happy days in the sunshine and, afterwards, in the cool of the evening, driving back home along country lanes white with cow parsley and the elms and the chestnuts green above us and an afterglow of sunset stretching far across the horizon.

All the youthful energy! Many times have I played cricket in an all day match until 6.30, on to play tennis with Margaret and our friends until dusk, walked to her home a mile or so across the city and, for good measure, walked home alone with Tim, in the dark, the further two miles that involved. The saying 'One is only young once' is very true!

But September would bring a chill into the air and, as in early spring, I would find myself rugged up on the boundary edge in two sweaters and even, for further insulation, wearing an old pair of pyjama legs under my flannels. Sadly we would play our last match. Sight screens would be pushed and stored by the pavilion, the square roped off and as we dispersed the ground was silent, deserted and forlorn. But I was not forlorn, for, apart from a spate of examinations at this time of the year, the rugger season loomed ahead on my horizon and I could look forward to playing through the winter with the Lichfield Club and, in between times, odd games of soccer for local junior sides.

The Lichfield Rugby Club had been formed only some ten years previously at the time the Grammar School changed its school playing code from the soccer of the past. Many of the masters from the school had been instrumental in the inauguration of the local club and continued as playing members. Consequently the club, at this period in the middle thirties, was almost a continuation of school games resulting in a strong combination which achieved a high standard of play and excellent results. I had a roving commission in this team as a 'loose forward' and ran with the threes on a dry day yet could seek the warmth of the scrum when it was snowing. This position was very prolific and it was in the 1935 season that I was chosen to play for the County. However, I understand the laws of the game have been changed about so much that 'loose' forwards can no longer operate. Also, at this time, an English International, Roy Leyland, was appointed to the Grammar School staff and, apart from helping us with our game, was able to gather an International Fifteen to play an exhibition match against us. This match could not be accommodated on our own ground on the Burton Old Road but was transferred to the better equipped one at Whittington Barracks.

* * * *

Quite often we dropped in at one of the local cinemas on a Saturday night after playing rugger in the afternoon. Unfortunately because of this and because of the limited space between the rows of seats I usually had severe bouts of cramp and had need to straighten my legs by standing up, but as this was not popular with those behind and I finished up walking up and down the gangway. However, as the house would be quite full, I would have to take care that no one slipped in and took my seat, especially as I had left Margaret sitting there on her own.

It was at this time that the Regal cinema had opened in Tamworth Street and we had been so thrilled with the sheer luxury of it. The wide expanse of carpets, the sophisticated lighting, the curtains sliding across the whole width of the auditorium, the spaciousness and the quality of the sound — for 'talkies' were well established by then. We had since early Charlie Chaplin days, attended the Old Palladium in Bore Street on quite a regular basis and had, therefore, grown up with the silent flickering screen, frequent breakdowns in the projector room and grand piano accompaniment from the bare boards of the stage with the addition of a trumpet for the more grandiose presentations and even a violin when 'Hearts and Flowers' was needed to emphasise the sad bits. Originally we were taken to the 'pictures' by our aunt who, if she thought there was something on the screen our young selves should not see, such as scenes in Dr. Fu Man Chu, covered our eyes with her hands. Even so we generally managed to see through the gaps between her fingers and keep in touch with what was going on. Gradually we were allowed to attend on our own. Occasionally we went on Saturday afternoons. The Palladium was usually full and we sat in the balcony mainly because our rivals from Sandford Street would be on the lower deck. But we were all as one with Rin Tin Tin and Douglas Fairbanks and against the villains who committed outrageous acts and how we all cheered with relief when a beleaguered garrison heard a bugle sound just over the distant horizon and the cavalry appeared, through the dust, in full charge! When rifles had such unerring aim that, each time fired, a Sioux Indian fell tumbling from his piebald horse. I think we laughed more easily in those days and Chaplin, Harold Lloyd and Buster Keaton could quickly set us going. There were also groans of dismay and disappointment when the hero, in the serial, found himself in a situation from which he could not possibly extricate himself and the screen flashed 'To be continued next week'!

* * * *

From a very early age we held an intense interest in the motor car which, then, were much more identifiable because of the shapes of the exposed

Dennis at the wheel of the old Swift

Cricket on the Tennis Lawn

Lichfield R.F.C. 1936
Dennis first left front, myself first left rear

Lichfield Cricket Club, 1936
Dennis second right front, myself second right rear

radiators. We had an ambition to see the racing cars at Brooklands but never achieved it and had to be content with press and radio reports and, visually, on the News Reels at the local cinema. Le Mans races were also followed keenly and Tim Birkin and S. C. H. Davis were very much our heroes when they won in the Bentleys. We took the same interest in the Isle of Man T.T. races in the years when Nortons won every year with Lucky Simpson, Geoff Duke, Graham and the others. Ramsey Hairpin, the Mountain, Governor's Bridge and other hazards on the course became household words to us.

With such associated interests we were lucky at home always to have some type of motorised conveyance to travel about locally. In the early days it was the old B.S.A. motorcycle combination which served us well but had so many disadvantages as regards comfort and protection from the elements. But it was fairly reliable and my father had driven it solo up to London for cup finals at Crystal Palace and Stamford Bridge. The bike eventually gave way to the inevitable Austin Seven. Our first trip in this was entirely exploratory it appeared. Maybe father's foot slipped off the small metal clutch pedal because it had such a very limited travel but whatever the reason the car, from the start, bounced high and continued to do so down the street combined with a succession of jerks forward of about a yard or so at a time, much in the manner of a kangaroo. Mother, in the passenger seat, merely sat hoping for better things but Dennis and myself could hardly suppress our laughter as we bounced up and down on the back seat. Someway down the street father regained control and we were able to proceed to our destination. But that was not quite all for in turning out of the farm we had been to visit, the car was reversed over the grass verging finishing up very adjacent to a barn window which immediately opened for the farmer's head to appear to see what was going on. After all these difficulties father played safe and forced the car into top gear and kept it there for the whole of the journey home.

Some years later his second car, a Swift Tourer, was a firm favourite with all of us and it was with this car that I learned to drive. The gear lever was on the right down by your leg and had a heavy gate change. This, we felt, was good for learning and we prided ourselves that we could make very silent clutchless gear changes. Driving tests had not been introduced at this time but, once father was satisfied that we were efficient and safe, he let us drive and, indeed, borrow the car for our own occasional needs.

But during most of my three years of pupilage I had a stroke of luck regarding a conveyance. John had purchased an attractive open Triumph Scorpian but, because he landed himself a job as far afield as Scotland, he left it at home and allowed me to run it in his absence. This I did with some relish and I was able, amongst other journeys, to encompass a wider field of lecture centres in relation to my engineering learning. And, of course, it was most useful for Margaret and myself and naturally, we made much of this good fortune and travelled about, we thought, in some style. And when Charlie Kunz, Gracie Fields or other favourite Music Hall stars were appearing at the Hippodrome in Birmingham or a Tom Walls - Ralph Lynn Farce was on at the Theatre Royal it was most convenient for us to nip over and take our places.

I remember a wedding we attended together in this car. It was held in a small country village, Hamstall Ridware, just north of Lichfield. It was a lovely day in midsummer and Margaret had, especially for the occasion, a new cream linen suit. Now the oil pressure of the car engine was indicated, not by the needle gauge of today, but by a small tell tale black button on the dashboard. If there was trouble the button came outwards. We drove up to the church in fine style but, unfortunately, something had gone wrong with the little button for it had discharged several drops of black oil downwards on the passenger side. To our joint horror as Margaret stepped from the car there was the tell tale oil on the front of her cream skirt. It didn't spoil the day but I cannot recall whether or not the costume ever regained acceptable cleanliness.

* * * *

Suddenly three years had passed quickly by. Three Bowers had come and gone. Spring each year had been as lovely as ever over in Leamonsley Wood. Through the autumns Margaret and myself had tramped across the stubble and turnip fields with Tim as usual, half a mile away scenting a pheasant. I had knocked half vollies past mid-off in summer sunshine and, on winter days, ran for the line, clear, for tries and a snow flurry would sweep across the ground as we converted. I had discussed the day gone with my parents over suppers late at night and we would sit and check my exam schedules and laugh together as I queried whether my allowance from the Council qualified for income tax.

Meanwhile, much had been going on in the world outside my local orbit. Stanley Baldwin was Prime Minister, we still had an Empire and J. B. Priestley was a young man. Malcolm Campbell achieved a land speed of 276 m.p.h. in Blue Bird on Daytona Beach and a horse called Reynoldstown won the Grand National two years in succession. Very high was our enthusiasm and pride when an Englishman, Fred Perry landed Wimbledon three times in a row and Henry Cotton the British Golf Open at Sandwich and Carnoustie. We followed intently the bodyline series in Australia and our passion had been raised in support of Jardine and Larwood yet when, in the same year, Hitler became Chancellor of Germany we took very little notice. In 1935 King George had his Silver Jubilee and we all gathered in the recreation grounds to see the fireworks and listen to the harmonies from the Cathedral Glee Singers wafting across to the fairy lights stretched out along Pool Walk, as they had done those years so long ago.

In the following year I had motored down to visit Dennis at his University and, in his room, we heard with askance the abdication speech on the radio and realised, slowly, the royal career of our hero, the Prince of Wales with which we had proudly grown up, was now at an end.

My pupilage was also nearing its end and I seemed to be progressing well and I was qualifying through the examinations. The time had arrived for me to be seeking a position elsewhere than in Lichfield. In 1937 such positions were not easy to find. Even then, as perhaps now, we tended first to search to the south and, if unsuccessful, settle for the north somewhere. After many fruitless attempts all over the country I landed a position in Lancashire. Everyone shared my delight. Yet, at that moment, it all seemed so strange for, whereas I had grown up near villages with names such as Kings Bromley, Farewell and Yoxall, the station name board at which I alighted, for my short list, proclaimed 'Moses Gate'. As the ticket collector clipped my return ticket I glanced outside and saw, not green grass and three graceful spires, but a cobbled street and high dark mill chimneys towering above me. A girl struggled by wearing clogs and a cream and blue tramcar careered and growled along the centre of the road on its way to Horwich, via Bolton.

Elmhurst Hall (now demolished)

Charges to pay
______s.______d.
RECEIVED

POST OFFICE TELEGRAM

No.______
• OFFICE STAMP

LICHFIELD 1 FE 37

Prefix. Time handed in. Office of Origin and Service Instructions. Words.

5.54 P m

From 2 — | 4 35 | Farnworth Bolton | 10 | To______

Brown 250 Beacon St
Lichfield
Have bought plus job
Cuth

For free repetition of doubtful words telephone "TELEGRAMS ENQUIRY" or call, with this form at office of delivery. Other enquiries should be accompanied by this form and, if possible, the envelope.

B & C

"Success" — there were very few 'phones in 1937

On Pipe Green with Margaret and Tim and the ever present Spires, 1937

On a Sunday morning a fortnight later I was on my way north again to take up my appointment. It was a bright morning in early February. I had taken Tim over Pipe Green for his morning run and, as he splashed along the brook, little did he know what was afoot. As we came back down the lane the bells of the Cathedral were spreading their message of Sabbath joy across the countryside.

My own and Margaret's father saw me off at Trent Valley Station and wished me success in the career upon which I was now embarking. As the signal dropped and the engine puffed and slid into motion their handshakes were warm and heartfelt. I hoisted my suitcase — a bright new leather one with my initials emblazoned on the side, a parting gift from recent office colleagues — on to the luggage rack and stood looking out of the window to watch the Cathedral Spires receding away across the vale and with the low winter sun glinting on the veins of their pinnacles. Soon, gathering speed, I realised we were nearing Elmhurst crossing and I looked over towards the cricket field where, in a match only last summer, we had scrambled the winning single in a failing light.

I knew this life known countryside about me was moving into the past yet I could not allow myself to be sad for a wider world than these local fields lay before me. I was setting out for my first job with satisfaction and excitement and, added to this, I already sensed a feeling of independence and, possibly, importance.

However, as I settled down with the Sunday paper, I suddenly realised I had meant to bring my bicycle with me and stow it into the luggage van but, in the flurry of last minute arrangements, I had forgotten all about it and left it at home. Obviously I was far from being infallible and, allowing myself a smile, hurriedly returned to my more normal self and the football results on the back page.